WORK, LOVE AND I

WORK, LOVE AND MARRIAGE

The Impact of Unemployment

Janet Mattinson

in collaboration with
Stan Ruszczynski
Diana Daniell
Nina Cohen

Duckworth

First published in 1988 by
Gerald Duckworth & Co. Ltd.
The Old Piano Factory
43 Gloucester Crescent, London NW1

ISBN 0 7156 2220 X (cased)
ISBN 0 7156 2230 7 (paper)

British Library Cataloguing in Publication Data

Mattinson, Janet
    Work, love and marriage
    1. Married couples. Interpersonal
    relationships
    I. Title
    306.8'72

    ISBN 0-7156-2220-X
    ISBN 0-7156-2230-7 Pbk

Photoset in North Wales by
Derek Doyle & Associates, Mold, Clwyd
Printed in Great Britain by
Unwin Brothers Limited, Old Woking

Contents

But they'll never listen. Maybe you'll not listen either, but I'm telling you it started on that cold January evening when Dad came home from work.

He wasn't walking properly. He held onto the edge of the door, and then onto the sideboard, and he walked very very slowly to his chair, as if he was drunk. I thought he was drunk. He had a letter in his hand. That was about six o'clock. Then Chunder came round about an hour later, and Dad had never moved from his chair, and he hadn't touched the mug of tea I'd made for him ...

I thought there was some funeral on or something, but I didn't know what I was seeing – just my old man come home from work and Chunder round visiting.

Janni Howker, *The Nature of the Beast*, 1985

Foreword

Society is changing faster than ever before. Change which affects both paid employment and unpaid household work makes us uncomfortably aware of how our very ideas of manhood and womanhood have been structured by our work roles. Marriage itself has been patterned by the routines and rhythms of the two separate spheres.

Until recently, no book would have tried to combine a study of the sociology of work and marriage with a psychodynamic analysis of marital relations. In *Work, Love and Marriage*, Janet Mattinson has done just this; and it is a sign of the times in which we live that nothing less would do justice to the topic. Our accustomed separation of the disciplines of social science has been breaking down, along with the separation of the spheres of social life.

She and her colleagues have studied couples in which the man was unemployed, and the process of helping them with marital problems. The conclusions they draw are wide-ranging – about the relationship between love and work, about intimacy and emotional distance, and about society's defences against the painful facts of unemployment. They draw on perspectives as apparently divergent as psychoanalysis and Marxism.

The result is a book which is both stimulating and disturbing. Like other pioneering books, it crosses boundaries and questions established demarcations. It explores the way in which the individual unconscious is structured by social forces, and how economic and power relations can therefore 'get inside' people, affecting their deepest experiences of meaning and despair.

Social workers, counsellors, doctors and clergy all struggle to help people whose problems are as much about economic change and social upheaval as they are about psychological distress. This book will help them see what they have previously missed, and relate what they previously kept separate.

W.J.O. Jordan
Reader in Social Studies
Exeter University

Preface

I bear final responsibility for the form and style of this book, but I was one member of a project team with three of my colleagues: Stan Ruszczynski, Diana Daniell and Nina Cohen. We all worked as therapists with couples in the clinical sample. Diana and Stan were leaders of the pilot workshop in London, and they and I were designated leaders of the workshops in Devon and Tyneside from which much of our material is drawn. Nina joined us in Devon when one of our co-group leaders fell ill. She was also in charge of the figures in Appendix I. Diana developed a particular interest in the meaning of work, and Part I of the book draws on her material. Part III of the book draws on Stan's special interest in the problems of working with unemployed people. At our weekly project meeting we discussed, argued and even fought over early drafts. Benita Dyal was our most able project secretary and responsible for the final processing of the text. In this way the book belongs to us all.

Other colleagues in the Institute of Marital Studies supported us, criticised and commented, but we want to thank Warren Colman for the detailed attention he gave to the drafts. Margaret Walker and her staff in the Tavistock Centre Library serviced us with their usual efficiency and interested involvement.

On the workshops in Devon and Tyneside we invited senior practitioners of the local services to co-lead the groups with us to keep us in touch with local conditions and constraints. In both areas we formed a stimulating staff group. On the basis that, if staff are learning, there is a chance of members doing likewise, we thank them for their lively contributions: in Devon, Claire Shimmell, Tony Lovewell and Carl Buttle; in Tyneside, Gill Birkby, Bridget Hester and John Lowen. We thank all the members of these workshops – social workers, probation officers, health visitors, marriage guidance counsellors and pastoral counsellors – who are listed in Appendix III.

Through the good offices of Jean Packman, the University of Exeter hosted the Devon workshop. The Northumbria Probation Service helped us in the administration of the Tyneside workshop. Tony Bray and Gill Birkby were our chief liaison officers.

The project would not have been possible without the generous financial support of St Luke's College Foundation, the Millfield House Foundation, the Northumbria Probation Service and one other Trust remaining anonymous. The Institute of Marital Studies, which receives its major grant from the Home Office, also contributed to the cost.

We thank Julia MacRae Books and Janni Howker for permission to quote from *The Nature of the Beast*; Faber and Faber for permission to use an extract from Douglas Dunn's short story, 'Getting Used to it', in *Secret Villages*; and Quartet Books for extracts from Mervyn Jones' *Holding On*.

As always with this type of book, our major debt is to the patients and clients who, by telling us what it was like for them, taught us – their pupils. In their interest they remain anonymous behind their pseudonyms and some altered identifying factors.

Finally, I thank Bill Wallis for his comments and help with the final draft and, more important, for bearing with me through the preoccupation which this type of project and writing engenders – some chapters even going on holiday with us – and all of it as I approached my own unemployment/ retirement. This, I am sure, was no coincidence.

J.M.

Introduction

This world's no blot for us,
Nor blank; it means intensely, and means good:
To find its meaning is my meat and drink.
                                        Robert Browning

This book is about interaction. In describing and analysing the psychological impact of unemployment on some married couples and on practitioners (therapists, social workers, probation officers, health visitors, marriage guidance counsellors and pastoral counsellors) who attempted to help these couples, it focusses on the interaction between husbands and wives; on the relationship between employment and domestic satisfaction or dissatisfaction; on the link between the unemployment of one partner and what was often a changed marital relationship; and on the interaction between unemployed clients and employed practitioners.

Inevitably this book is also about loss: the loss of job and all which that entails. For many unemployed people the losses encompass

Ways of defining self
Ways of acquiring status
Means of exercising skill and sense of achievement
or
Simple endurance of monotonous drudgery or robot-like activity
Means of organising time and structuring the day
Means of finding companionship
Means of obtaining expected level of income
and for those on benefit
Adequate income and consumer power

In addition, this book is about meanings which may be quite conscious, barely conscious, or deeply unconscious; for example, the meaning of what is lost both for the loser and the

1

loser's partner beyond (or should we say, below) the obvious losses listed above. It is about the relationship between the meaning of the lost job and the meaning of the marriage – why a couple chose each other in the first place and, in some instances, the significance of the partner's occupation in that choice.

Most of the couples whom we describe grew up or worked for many years in a period of high employment. For a man, obtaining and remaining in paid work was assumed to be a fact of life. When work becomes unavailable, a massive adaptation is required of a couple in the view they hold of themselves and in the way they handle their domestic situation. That the couples in our sample asked for help, or were seen to require it by attracting attention to themselves, indicated that either they were unable to make an adaptation which satisfied them both, or, as it seemed to others, the adaptation they made was not good enough.

Most of them were casualties of technological, economic and social change. The way people respond to change not of their own making depends on the external resources available to them (including the way they are treated) and their own internal resources, physical, mental and emotional. For example, the word 'redundant', defined in the *Concise Oxford Dictionary* as *superfluous*, rebounds much more on the inner world of a person who lacks confidence in his innate lovableness than of a person who is sure of his own worth. The latter person may be severely shaken in his belief that he is not superfluous, but by the nature of that belief he has the basic resource with which to recover.

We firmly believe that people are at their happiest, strongest and most creative when the external world confirms their best and most hopeful images, or they are able to transform the external reality through their own symbolism to fit these images; and that they are at their most miserable, disturbed and weakest when the world confirms their worst fears about themselves. We state this belief from our position as marital psychotherapists in the Institute of Marital Studies (IMS) which offers a therapeutic service to couples who are experiencing difficulties in their relationship. As therapists using psychoanalytic ideas, we are concerned with people's inner worlds and the meaning to them of those people with whom they choose to be in close association. Many of the factors which determine the formation of a close relationship are often clearly perceived: 'I love him because...' Other factors are operative at an unconscious level of the mind – the indefinable 'It' of the in-love state. We do not distinguish unconscious factors as of a different order of thought or feeling from conscious ones. Some people are more reflective than others about their own behaviour (and that of others) and make connections between some of their actions and less obvious feelings and earlier experiences in their lives. What is consciously motivated for one person may be quite unconscious for another.

The project

Some years ago we became aware from a few instances in our clinical work, that even when optional redundancy had been chosen, the partners were often shocked by their reaction and by the exposure of a marital problem, which either had existed before the redundancy and was exacerbated by it, or had arisen directly from the changed circumstances. A previously virile husband became impotent. A wife, carrying high status in her own employment, could neither bear the loss of her husband's status, nor her becoming the sole earner, nor the required shift in domestic roles.

The IMS is also a training and research establishment. It trains specialist and non-specialist practitioners in marital counselling, placing emphasis not so much on particular techniques, as on increasing understanding of processes of interaction in marital relationships and marital problems. Its action research and development projects always relate to the practice of counselling within different settings. The findings of these projects, like the staff's own clinical work, inform the teaching.

As the unemployment figures rose nationally (between 1979 and 1984, the number rose by 2 million; between 1983 and 1984 long term (more than one year) unemployment increased by 15%[1]), it became important to us to know if and how patients and clients were presenting marital and family problems related to the unemployment of one or both partners to other professional helpers; whether these practitioners were responding to this particular need; and whether detailed clinical insights which we were starting to develop could be of use to them in making more effective responses than they might otherwise do.

In 1984 we embarked on a project which had two spheres of operation: clinical work in the IMS; and workshops with other practitioners in a range of settings in three parts of the country, which would enable us to put our experience alongside theirs.

The clinical sample

We already had experience of some couples in therapy who had been affected by redundancy either before they applied for help or during the process of therapy. They formed the basis of a sample and we decided to take active steps to see more couples who were facing these circumstances.

Couples can refer themselves directly to the IMS, and over 50% do so. The majority of the formally referred come via their general medical practitioner (GP). Many marital problems for which help is sought are, in the first instance, presented to GPs and not to the specialist agencies.[2] These problems are not always presented directly. Physical and mental symptoms are used as signals of underlying unhappiness. A discerning GP can sometimes involve the partner and help a couple to redefine the problem in terms of their relationship.[3]

We informed our regular referrers in Greater London and the Home Counties (the IMS has no catchment area) that we were particularly interested in receiving referrals of couples in which one partner was unwillingly unemployed; that such couples would receive an immediate vacancy; and fees, always negotiable according to income, would be rescinded for those with no income other than state benefit.

It was in subsequent months that we started to come up against what we later defined as one of our major findings. *Many people do not want to know about the reality of the adverse effects of unemployment on others.* In what now seems to have been a naive attitude we expected, not to be deluged, but, at least, to receive a slow, steady response to our request. We were wrong in our expectation. When, at our next regular meeting with our referrers, we again drew attention to our requirements and wondered why they had not responded, they told us that they had very few unemployed patients on their lists. One GP, working in an East End borough of London, actually maintained that he had *no* unemployed patients. As at that time the unemployment rate in South East England was 9.3% and in that particular borough 22%, we were, to put it mildly, surprised.

We knew from the literature that statistically the unemployed have more than their fair share of mental and physical symptoms,[4] a higher than normal suicide rate,[5] and a higher divorce rate than the employed.[6] However, we also knew that amongst the few couples we already had in treatment the actual unemployment was sometimes denied by the unemployed person. In one instance we learnt about a recent redundancy only from the spouse. Mr Astor assured his wife and the therapists (in the IMS two therapists work with each couple) that he was now self-employed, although there was no evidence that he had any actual work. Mr Clarke, previously earning well, refused the offer of a negotiated lower fee. He would soon be back in paid employment at a comparable salary, he maintained. Despite his efforts, he was not. Only several months later was he able to accept the reality of his situation. Perhaps, we wondered, patients were not telling their GPs that they were unemployed.

We called a special meeting of representatives of several services to see if they could help us to understand why it was proving so difficult to collect an adequate clinical sample. Among the various ideas put forward, the most meaningful was what we came to call the 'not rocking the boat' syndrome: a shocked, suddenly redundant husband was often treated by his wife as an excessively vulnerable victim who must not be upset any more than he was already. Issues in the couple's way of relating, accentuated by the unemployment of one of them, could not be openly tackled while one remained a victim. When the world of work had collapsed, it was too threatening for both husband and wife to acknowledge the possibility of further collapse at home.

After this meeting we decided to increase the advertisement of the service we were offering. We displayed what we thought was an appealing and sensitively illustrated poster in Job Centres, Public Libraries, GP surgeries, Citizens' Advice

Bureaux and Social Services Offices in the immediate neighbourhood. As far as we know, it occasioned no response. None of the self-referred in the final sample told us that they had come because they had seen the poster. Some months later we were advised that our poster might have been more effective if, although still placed in Job Centres, and still offering help for marriage problems, it had not mentioned the word *unemployed*.

Our sample grew slowly, the fact of one partner being unemployed seemingly incidental in the mind of the referrer or the self-referred to the marital problem about which they told us.

At the time we started to write this book, our clinical sample, collected over three years, numbered 25. Formally it consists of couples of whom one or both partners were made redundant or, given a choice, took redundancy or early retirement *and* sought help for a marital problem either before or after the employment of the husband or wife ceased. In fact, in all cases, it was the husband's pending or actual unemployment or the husband's and wife's unemployment which brought them into the sample, never just the wife's unemployment.

The length of the period of unemployment varied from two months to over three years. The ages ranged from 28 to 59 years. The majority of couples, as in the IMS patient-population as a whole, were in Social Class II with professional or managerial qualifications. The couples were in therapy for different lengths of time ranging from a brief consultation to several weeks, months or even years. Appendix I gives further details of ages, social class, lost occupations and length of unemployment.

The meaning of work

One outcome of our therapeutic work with the first few couples who entered our clinical sample was a growing interest in, and recognition of, the need to understand the particular meaning of the nature of the job which has previously been held and then lost.

As marital therapists, we already knew that it was difficult to understand the individual meaning of a separation or divorce for distressed, deserted spouses, if we did not first acquire some understanding of the very personal meaning of the marriage which initially had been entered with hope and love. What were the conscious and unconscious preoccupations which drew a couple together? What element of the original betrothal had been betrayed and left them feeling so devastated?

In similar terms, we needed to learn the meaning or psychological purpose of one job, rather than another, for an individual and his spouse beyond the obvious functions listed on p.1 – self-definition, status, use of skill, structured time and ready-made opportunity for some social intercourse – if we were to acquire more understanding of the impact when that job was lost.

In the belief that patients are the best teachers – better than any technical book – and following our usual way of enquiry, asking them to *tell us*, we started to listen more carefully than we had done in the past to what people told us about their previous jobs. We listened for the meaning of those jobs in their inner and private world. What, apart from the list of general functions, had been lost along with the job? How major a part had it played in, for example, shoring up a weak sense of identity? What expression had it given to a personality characteristic? What were the implications of there now being only a domestic avenue for expression of this characteristic; the sergeant major controlling the family as he had controlled the troops; the teacher unable to refrain from teaching; the competitive manager now competing only with his wife?

Our increased interest in the meaning of different types of jobs for different types of people, often at an unconscious level, started to affect our work with employed couples not in the project sample. We had been aware for many years that marital therapy with a couple often resulted in a more effective or relaxed performance at work on the part of the husband before it enabled him to modify his behaviour at home; with wives, it is usually the other way round. Now we started to listen with a more informed ear to what people told us about their paid employment. We pricked up our ears, for example, when Mrs Young, unprompted by the therapists, said to her architect husband, 'It's strange, but I have just realised that we're always going on about space and quarrelling about space one way or another – where to put this, how to arrange that and whether there's enough room for this or that; and when you're designing, you're still ordering space on your drawing board.'

When we were discussing our project with a group of medical officers working in industrial and business firms, we talked of the relationship between some illnesses and some occupations and the type of body image that seemed to be held in certain occupations. We were interested to learn that the Post Office does not need to exercise undue concern about postmen's feet! Apparently men and women who apply for this job usually see themselves as good walkers and are not normally troubled by corns, bunions or flat feet.

And we learnt of the problem in some areas where, for example, steel works had closed and light industry opened; but it was the wives of the steel workers who applied for the new jobs. Were the steel workers' hands too big and rough to work with nylon? Or were these jobs too 'cissy' for large, strong men and incompatible with their image of masculinity?

This type of conversation led us, who were concerned with marriage relationships, to think about the meaning of a job for the worker's partner. Mrs Chambers, with artistic ability but inhibited from using it, acquired considerable satisfaction when she married a man pursuing an artistic career.

We suggest that when jobs are readily available, choice of occupation or a person's finally settling in one job rather than another is of psychological relevance; that type of work, its degree of structure and its conditions, provide a vehicle whereby inner, often unconscious preoccupations can be worked at and sometimes resolved or made less burdensome. As therapists, we are aware of what our patients, their illnesses and their problems do for us; in trying to help them, we often succeed in helping ourselves. The author did well for her own sense of deprivation when she worked as a child care officer, sometimes rescuing, sometimes placing children for fostering or adoption, at times helping to keep families together. In her youth, she firmly believed she could put the world of deprivation to rights in one county borough. Having put something to rights for herself, but remaining confused about her intelligence, she somehow managed to get herself a job in a university. Her first piece of research was on couples who had been designated subnormal. She learnt that many of these couples were not nearly as dull as the labelling suggested, nor she as dense as she used to suppose.

When jobs are not so readily available and choice cannot be exercised, a job tells us less about the person who holds it. However, when people have to take jobs which do not suit their psychological preoccupation, or which are even antithetical to them, substantiating destructive as opposed to creative, healing images, they will be not just bored, but unduly stressed.

This book, originally intended to be simply about loss of employment and the effect of this on some marriages, is also about paid work and the meaning of work. We took this new interest into the second sphere of the project.

The workshops

Within our training programme, we offer courses and workshops. If it is a course that is on offer, there is an assumption that we have something distinctive to sell to the membership from our specialised knowledge. If a workshop is on offer, we, as leaders, want to learn as much from the members as they may do from us. With them, we wanted to explore some particular area of work and put their experience alongside ours – a joint endeavour.

We planned to offer three workshops in different parts of the country: a pilot one in London, consisting of ten weekly seminars; and two more substantial ones in contrasting areas in which unemployment was near or above the national average. We chose to go to areas in which we already had contacts and where our style and quality of work was already known. We negotiated and set up workshops in Devon (1984 unemployment rate 12.9%) and North Tyneside (1984 unemployment rate 18.7%). The one in Devon was hosted by the University of Exeter. The Northumbria Probation Service played a major part in the initial administration and involvement of other services in the Tyneside region.

The three workshops were interdisciplinary and a number of places were allocated to each local service: Marriage Guidance, Social Services, Probation, Health Visiting, General Practice and the Church. Despite both Exeter and Newcastle being centres for the training of GPs, the medical profession did not take up any places. Because of the exploratory nature of the event, fees were not charged, but employers were contributing their officers' time, travelling and subsistence expenses.

The workshops in Devon and Tyneside, like many other events in our training programme, were of a sandwich nature with three parts. Part I consisted of a block period of a week in which we and the members worked together and shared experiences and ideas. Much of the work was done in small groups and focussed on the detailed case material of the members. In some plenary sessions, we offered some structured input from our own experience and pulled some threads together from the work in the small case discussion groups. At the end of each day we re-assembled in small groups to take stock of where we had reached and of the sometimes uncomfortable feelings which had been evoked, either by the substance of some of the case material or by an intensive learning experience. This is our usual practice on courses and workshops. Taking the temperature, clearing the air, and sometimes becoming conscious of the underlying mood of the groups at repeated intervals enables the work to be pursued more diligently than it otherwise might be.

In Part II, members returned to their regular work in their own services for a period of three months to test out and utilise ideas acquired in Part I. In Part III, we all met again for a further week to share this experience and, in the light of this, to take our ideas further forward. We believe that the opportunity to refute, modify or confirm ideas allows greater scope for creative and imaginative thinking which remains firmly grounded in reality than one-off events.

In Appendix II there is a copy of the circulated leaflet which described a proposed workshop and invited application. Appendix III lists the membership of the three workshops.

However, the Tyneside workshop was not fully subscribed. The vacancies surprised us as preliminary correspondence and meetings with managers of departments had elicited con-siderable interest. In an area where our work was known and at a time when training monies were severely restricted, we were offering a free event with an in-built training component on a subject which, we thought, must be of central relevance to most staff working in this area. Having widened the catchment area we were still undersubscribed. When we queried the complete lack of applications from one Probation Department, we were told by the Assistant Chief Probation Officer that he was as disappointed as we were; he had circulated the notice twice with no response – not a flicker of interest – and yet 74% of the total departmental caseload was unemployed.

Obviously many factors were operating in different services which affected the response rate. Whereas in Devon, for example, Marriage Guidance had taken up its full allocation, in the north-east most counsellors were in full-time employment and could not take time off for study relating to their voluntary work. No doubt there were many other pressing problems preoccupying workers in all services. We wondered whether in an area of such pervasive unemployment the subject had become 'old hat'. We learnt that when a one-day workshop had been offered in the area two years previously, it had been oversubscribed. A repeat or continuation had been requested for the following year. This had not taken place because the earlier enthusiasm had evaporated.

However, we had already learnt from our pilot workshop in London that the phenomenon of denial mentioned earlier in this chapter operated among the helping professions generally; it was not just the GPs who did not want to know. We had learnt that many practitioners when taking an initial case history would tick the unemployment box (just as private or council housing would be noted), but only as a basic fact of life, and not one justifying further enquiry into the client's feelings, detailed circumstances, or as having relevance to the offence or other type of presented problem. Why, we asked, when social workers and counsellors are able to relate to the desperately sad circumstances of many of their clients, can they not relate to this particular one? Why was the subject so unpopular? Was it particularly difficult for the employed to help the unemployed?

We also wondered whether the subject was too 'close to the bone' for some practitioners, for by this time social services were facing cuts. Unemployment was not unknown in the helping professions.

Not surprisingly, some of those who responded to the invitation to join the workshops had themselves been unemployed or had children who were so. They had a personal as well as a professional investment in understanding more about the complex nature of the feelings they had or were experiencing in their private life. We in the IMS were similarly affected, as the IMS, a voluntary body, has throughout its history often been under threat of closure. At the time we embarked on this project, we felt under greater threat than ever before and we all knew that the size of the staff might have to be reduced. We ourselves knew about the threat, if not the actuality, of being unemployed.

We are citizens as well as therapists and, as citizens, we have our own political views. This project was different from any others we had previously undertaken in that it had huge political dimensions. Our workshops needed to take account of this, and plenary sessions and end of day stock-taking groups needed to allow space for it.

As on many of our teaching or project events, we also needed to work with the institutions seconding staff as well as with individual workers. Time is ill-spent in helping practitioners to increase their understanding and to modify certain aspects of their work, if the organisation does not take into account that changed practice often requires changed institutional frameworks. At the end of the Devon and Tyneside workshops we met with representatives of the managers of the different services. We put back to them some of the findings and we engaged with them in discussion of some of the issues as they saw them from their wider managerial perspective.

The sample of cases acquired from the workshops, defined like those in the clinical sample – at least one partner of the marriage unwillingly unemployed – numbered 34. Except in one case, it was the husband's, not the wife's, unemployment which brought a couple into the sample. In one case both husband and wife were unemployed. The period of unemployment had lasted from less than six months to over four years. The ages ranged from 24 to 57 years. There was a wider spread of social class than in the clinical sample with a predominance of Social Classes III and V, giving us overall a representation of all social class groups as defined by the Registrar General. Appendix I gives details of the workshop sample alongside the clinical one.

*

This book uses material from our IMS clinical sample and from cases presented in the workshops. Identifying characteristics are excluded or altered. In Appendix I there is a list of actual lost occupations. In the text an occupation is sometimes altered in the interests of confidentiality, although the alternative occupation is always of a similar nature and status and has similar training requirements. Pseudonyms are used. In the IMS sample they start with a letter from A to H; in the workshop sample from J to T. The name of one couple not formally included in the workshop sample, but affected by the threat of redundancy which then did not occur, starts with a W. A few other couples not in either sample, but from whose circumstances brief illustrative material is used, have a pseudonym starting with Y.

We have not used all the couples in the two samples for illustrative material. Too many examples can bore and confuse the reader. If one couple, already used for this purpose, will illustrate a later point, they are used again, so that some couples reappear throughout the book. Readers can, if they choose, trace a couple through the index of clients. However we do not want readers to think they need to remember a couple from one chapter to the next. Enough descriptive material is given on each occasion to make sense of the point and to help recall for those who want to keep the connection.

The book is in three main parts which reflect the specialist interests which three of us developed during the course of the project. Part I, 'Love and Work', draws on Diana Daniell's study of these two aspects of life which she increasingly understood as complementary aspects of identity.[7] It explores the psychological purpose of some types of occupation which have relevance to the interactive system set up between married partners and to their sense of well-being or stress. It shows how some jobs and some marriages are used to contain or heal old wounds and vulnerabilities, sometimes the job and the marriage supporting each other, sometimes conflicting with each other, in the task. As psychodynamic therapists we are particularly concerned with intimate psychological processes, but we set employment, love and marriage as we know them today in their economic, social, historical and wider psychological context.

Part II, 'Loss of Work', (which became the author's chief interest) is about the effects this loss may have on some marriages, both by engendering problems, and by accentuating existing ones in the relationship. It discusses the weight of grief involved in loss of job and the complexity of the mourning process after this loss; and it describes the changed patterns of marital interaction that most commonly occurred in the families in our samples.

Part III, 'Employed to help the Unemployed', became Stan Ruszczynski's main interest. Chapter 8, 'Under the Influence', describes some of the problems we and the members of the workshops encountered when working with unemployed couples. In Chapter 9, 'The Management of Change', we look at the wider social and political context in which this professional relationship takes place. In the final section of that chapter, 'Ill-fare or Welfare?', we argue for a more active concept of welfare than the outdated one currently in use, based as it is on an image of industrial man. A new concept of welfare needs to take account of a changing economic and social world.

We emphasise that we have not attempted to measure, nor to predict. We have not controlled our samples with a group who have not asked for help or a group who had not been affected by unemployment. Clinical insights such as we offer in this book will, hopefully, alert other practitioners in the helping professions to be more responsive and attentive to what their clients might tell them if given the opportunity, and provide ideas that may help them to make sense of what are often immensely complex motives and patterns of behaviour.

'They were ideas,' said the philosopher firmly, 'rudimentary ideas. All thought, in its early stages, begins as action. The actions which you have been wading through have been ideas, clumsy ones of course, but they had to be established as a foundation before we could begin to think in earnest.'

T.H. White, *The Book of Merlin*

PART I

LOVE AND WORK

He was fucking her, surely, as a husband fucks his wife. It was deep and close, and always it reached through time, forward and back. It had a quick hastening rhythm within itself, and a long swaying rhythm outside itself. He felt these two rhythms in fucking as he felt them in work. He stacked a hold with the sureness gained in other holds, and finished it as a link to other ships yet on the seas or yet unbuilt. ... A man's life was made in his work and in his woman – what else?

Mervyn Jones, Holding On

1

Purpose and Meaning

It is about a search for daily meaning as well as daily bread, for recognition as well as cash, for astonishment rather than torpor, in short for a sort of life rather than sort of dying.

Terkel

Without in any way purporting to be philosophers, most people expect to find some purpose and meaning in their lives, to feel they are realising themselves as individuals and social creatures, or, as we might say, *to make a living* in the fullest sense of the word.

Making a living can be done at different levels according to the natural, social and economic environment. When conditions are severe, the purpose of survival reigns supreme; all effort is put into remaining alive. When physical danger is not imminent and survival in terms of food and shelter is assured, certain aspects of humanity which distinguish human beings from other organisms seek expression; use of intelligence and mastery of skills not required for saving and maintaining life at its barest level can be harnessed to a range of pursuits, activities and achievements. Maslow has placed different levels of human needs and their drive for expression in a 'hierarchy of need'.[1] With fear of losing life less paramount, the human capacity for a wide range of feelings, many of which will conflict, can also seek expression: the need for love, affection and a sense of belonging; at a yet higher level, the need for esteem, reputation and prestige; and finally the need for self fulfilment to become more and more what one is capable of becoming and, in doing so, integrate different aspects of personality into a coherent whole.

Self-fulfilment in making a living presupposes a sense of self. Despite the fact that human beings are essentially social animals and cannot survive and develop in isolation, and strive

17

intensely for relationships with one another, part of the extraordinary phenomenon of humanity is the unique Gestalt of each individual and the potential capacity to experience a sense of self.

Identity as a concept is elusive, just as, or because, the individual's sense of identity can be elusive, never gained or maintained once and for all. As Erikson[2] has stated, identity can be only too conscious, but we are most aware of it when we are just about to gain it or about to enter a crisis which threatens it. At other times it is less conscious and experienced as a sense of psychosocial wellbeing. When relatively well developed, its most obvious concomitants are a feeling of being 'at home' in one's own body, a sense of knowing where one comes from and where one is going, of an inner coherence (that is, a relatively well integrated personality) and an inner assuredness of anticipated recognition from those who count. As Strauss has said, 'Whatever else it may be, identity is connected with the fateful appraisals made of oneself – by oneself and by others.'[3] Ironically, it needs to be at its strongest when a person is in close and intimate relationship with another, as in these circumstances fusion or diffusion of identity is most likely to occur. Strictly speaking, one can relate only from a point of difference and delineation.

That which can seek expression and be realised by an individual in promoting his sense of self and meaning of self depends on a basic human drive towards maturation and innate endowment which includes a range of levels of intelligence and sensibility. It also depends on what Hartman has called an 'average expectable environment'.[4] Erikson, using this phrase, emphasises the need for continuity: 'an "average expectable" continuity'. The readiness of the infant to grow physically, intellectually and emotionally according to a basic ground plan by pre-determined stages requires, he says, 'not only one basic environment, but a whole chain of successive environments'. As he grows physically, mentally and emotionally, it can be said that he has a claim to the next expectable environment.[5] The innate growth process does not realise itself without that environment which needs to contain, stimulate and encourage.

Environments fail children and adults, on the one hand because of tragedies, circumstances beyond human control, lack of knowledge and of resources, and on the other hand because of human frailty, error and inability to handle the darker side of human nature. A wide range of studies of child and adult development, failure of development, mental breakdown or psychological impairment (with varying theoretical bases) indicate the importance of early environments in establishing adult health and performance.[6] Gross failure of early environments to contain, stimulate and encourage the natural growth process leaves its scars. Relationships and attitudes established early in life set the pattern for the making of future relationships and productive activity which then either give meaning to an individual life or fail to do so. This is not to say that failure of environments required in adult life does not have severe effects on the individual, but simply that the stronger the foundations, the fewer the deep-seated scars, the greater the resilience in later life. Psychoanalytic studies of human development emphasise how conflicts in the very earliest relationships of life, which may get repressed and remain unconscious, continue to determine much adult behaviour, sometimes seemingly irrational, sometimes not so when harnessed in socially acceptable forms.[7]

From our particular stance as psychoanalytically orientated marital therapists, we want to emphasise our belief that unless or until all hope is killed off by a series of dire environments, the innate psychological growth process continues to seek expression and realisation throughout life; that the individual, propelled by this innate growth process, *seeks to heal old psychological wounds and to correct earlier unsatisfactory experiences.* In attempting to do this, he is living his life – that is, he has not given up the fight of life as he seeks personal, psychological meaning for himself. And, as part of this attempt to live his life, *he seeks, knowingly or unknowingly, a series of settings in which he can tangle with, and hope to master, his own internal psychological problems.*

Two spheres of life ('expectable environments') which can, but may not necessarily serve him in this quest are, first, outside the home, the environment of employment in which labour is exchanged for money. It is a highly organised world with massive power structures and, although dependent on co-operative effort, is often more characterised by competition and conflict. And second, inside the home, is the intimate and

domestic environment of marriage, procreation and parenthood. This is a world of unpaid work, mainly the wives'
prerogative. Although it is never free of competitive and
conflicting interests, it is normally approached with an
expectation of sharing and mutual exchange of services and
benefits, 'the harsh world of the market place ... softened by
bonds of love and friendship'.[8] Both spheres have the basic
purpose of maintaining life – fundamental dimensions of man's
existence. Together they fill a major part of life; both require
commitment; both can give opportunity for use of body, hand
and brain; and both can touch on or serve a wide range of
feeling. Each sphere impinges on and can be much influenced
by the other. Marriage and family life is especially vulnerable
to pressures and insecurities in the changing social and
economic organisation of which it is a part; undue stress at
work reverberates on family life. Similarly, performance at
work outside the home is manifestly affected by domestic and
emotional security or insecurity, satisfaction or lack of
satisfaction, at home.

When Freud was once asked what he thought a normal
person should be able to do well, he replied simply, 'Lieben und
arbeiten' ('to love and to work'). In talking of love, he was
speaking of 'the expansiveness of generosity as well as genital
love'. In talking of love and work, he was speaking of 'a general
work productiveness which would not preoccupy the individual
to the extent that his right or capacity to be a sexual and a
loving being would be lost.'[9]

In this part of the book, we look at these two spheres of life
which in our present society are still considered to be
'expectable environments' in which people can support
themselves and their families as social and individual beings,
and at the same time, in seeking to repair and make better
what was felt to be wrong in the past, find purpose and
meaning in their individual lives. We look at the struggle that
some couples in our samples have had, their successes and
partial successes, and their defeats and failures occasioned
either by the severity of their own problems and what is in
need of repair, or by the shortcomings or absence of a normal
'expectable environment'. First we look at the environment of
work, 'the most universally performed activity',[10] and place it
in its historical and social context.

2

Making a Living

The truth is that when a human being is not eating, drinking, sleeping, making love, talking, playing games or merely lounging about – and these things will not fill up a lifetime – he needs work and usually looks for it, though he may not call it work. Life has got to be lived largely in terms of effort. For man is not, as the vulgar hedonists suppose, a walking stomach; he has also got a hand, an eye and a brain. Cease to use your hand and you have lopped off a huge chunk of consciousness.

George Orwell

The fact is that after I felt sure of myself as a welder, I felt sure of myself in everything, even the way I walked.

Primo Levi

Toil

We can be certain that from the beginning of time man has worked (expended energy), often toiled, to maintain his and others' lives. As Marx and Engels pointed out, 'He distinguished himself from animals as soon as he began to produce his own means of subsistence.'[1] And, as Pope John Paul II said, in using hand and brain, man has transformed nature, harnessed its resources and adapted it to his needs. Through the centuries he has laboured to better the circumstances of life 'through a monumental amount of individual and collective effort'. He has been the heir to the work of previous generations and shared in the building of the future for the next generation.[2]

We can be less certain of the history of work, but attitudes to it seem to have altered through the centuries and varied from one culture to another. In the ancient world work was seen as a tedious activity not to be taken seriously.[3] Plato considered that citizenship should be restricted to a class of privileged persons, the sordid job of working to slaves and foreigners.[4] Aristotle also showed a contempt for the useful.[5] The less elevated Athenians, most of them tradesmen, artisans or farmers, thought it absurd to regard work as an end in itself; to work for wages would put the citizen in the position of the slave, whereas their aim in life was to preserve their full personal liberty and freedom of action.[6] A distinction was made between proper and improper work. Monotonous activity at a desk was considered more menial than that of the rough-clad artisan.[7]

Nearer home, mediaeval women in Britain would have been surprised to learn that a few hundred years later 'work' would be defined as employment and become the prerogative of one gender; that their married female descendants would, after the introduction of cotton and coal burning ranges and the new emphasis on cleanliness, be persuaded into the home and that their activity would not be considered to be work (as in the upper classes it was not, 'accomplishments' for women being more the order of the day). They might have been slightly less surprised that their female descendants would, before marriage, spearhead the development of an industrial workforce along with the Irish and other immigrants.

In pre-industrial England, economic partnership was a household strategy and the best use of resources for getting by. Although waged labour was universal for the poorest classes as early as the thirteenth century, those with moderate resources combined employment outside the household with work within it. Kinship groups exchanged labour services between households on a non-cash basis, the negotiations proving a source of quarrel and dispute as well as of assistance. Both men and women were active in the formal (cash) and informal (subsistence) parts of the economy. Women were productive in a variety of trades, their wages fluctuating similarly to those of men, but usually slightly higher.[8] However, 'the nearer the household was to the land, the stronger the tie between man and wife, the more nearly they were on equal terms.'[9]

There have been many different forms of work; new forms have appeared and other forms have disappeared. The industrial revolution dramatically changed the form, the place and the organisation of work for many people. Concentration of work in mills and factories and eventual exclusion of children, and then of women from heavy industry, isolated the father from his family. Grouping of mills and factories led to the concentration of much of the population in urban communities and 'the emergence of a self-conscious class of industrial workers'.[10] Much manual labour required in the earlier stages of the revolution has since been superseded by more and more perfected machines. More recent technologies in the electronics field (themselves the result of work as were the earlier machines) have revolutionised the style of work for many occupational groups. Service industries expanded by almost 2 million between 1971 and 1979 and following a slight contraction now account for 63.8% of the working population.[11]

One of the biggest historical changes in the pattern of work and, therefore, attitudes towards it, came with the increasing use of waged labour (employment) over the centuries. At first it was severely resisted. Strikes occurred in thirteenth-century France. In Britain, mediaeval 'St Monday' was much indulged to the fury of the masters, the worst offenders being the better paid. Much of the resistance was to the time-discipline. During the seventeenth and early eighteenth centuries, diversity and irregularity of the labour pattern was still the norm; mixed occupations, some waged labour along with some self-subsistence; alternate bouts of intense labour and enforced idleness which followed the seasons and often depended on the weather. Full employment was rare, under-employment, rather than cessation of work, being the main problem. An economy of dual, or even triple occupation, strengthened the position of the workforce and reduced reliance on wages.[12]

From the late eighteenth century, the change speeded up dramatically. With the industrial revolution and the rise of capitalism well under way, waged labour expanded. The labour force became subservient to the demands of capitalist enterprise. Many households became entirely dependent on a wage and other forms of customary work declined with one exception; women's work in the home expanded, but as women became more home-centred the family became more dependent on the man's wage. In some industrial towns there were few alternatives to the factory or steel works as a source of wage. As labour came to be used in an increasingly disciplined and specialised way, people became less variously skilled, their capacity to do other forms of work slowly whittled down.

Gradually, and then with a dramatic shift in the 1950s and 1960s, self-provisioning declined in favour of purchase. Women's work came to be seen as the provision of unpaid domestic and care services. They processed purchases rather than producing the basic commodities. They bought new equipment which created higher expectations of domestic hygiene and efficiency, but which did not always succeed in actually saving labour.

From 1955 to 1966 average weekly earnings including overtime increased by 130%. There were strong incentives for men to be employed for long hours, although often in an increasingly limited way (automation reducing the use of hand and brain) to earn the maximum amount of money to purchase the wealth of goods becoming more and more available. Local authority or privately rented housing left little scope or motivation for home improvement, and little space for horticultural activity. Long, time-disciplined hours of employment left little time for renovation or self-subsistence.

Another important change that accompanied the increasing use of waged labour over several centuries and the growing need for a disciplined but docile workforce in the factory was the elevation of work – an emergent ideology of the value of hard work to justify the increasing appropriation of one person's labour by another. Protestantism gave religious sanction both to the value of hard work and the pursuit of profit. Right up to the present day within and as a result of this capitalist ethos, the promotion of a work ethic, whether supported by religious asceticism or economic values, has dominated the social scene so that the non-worker – the idler – has been seen as delinquent or scrounging.

There was also a sharp differentiation between the expectations of men and women. Men were expected to realise themselves through their employment, preferably a career. Women were expected to embrace marriage and childbearing as a project and life plan; employment for them was to be a pre-marital time-filler and then a post-childbearing occupational therapy providing money for their own pocket or 'little extras' or luxuries for the family.

Right up to the middle of the twentieth century this ideology was not shared by the male labour force, recruited as it was from conditions of extreme poverty and without means of self-subsistence when driven off the land. 'Work was a means to an end, not an end in itself, and the end was survival in a hostile world which often seemed to deny even this modest ambition.'[13] Except for a minority – craftsmen who worked with pride or some of the less skilled who had some control and direction over their labour – work was not a central interest. 'For most it was taken as given, like life itself, to be endured rather than enjoyed',[14] as it was by many of their wives when they returned to work. More important were personal relationships with families, friends and workmates. Living and working at the same trade in the same area fostered tight-knit communities.

However, an extension of the ideology of work came after the second world war, and this did affect working-class life. Following a long period of deprivation, a new set of values emerged, focussed on psychological dimensions of life. The 'age of psychology',[15] as it has been called, promoted values of self-actualisation. The new values, along with those of the Welfare State which ensured survival, affected many areas of life.[16]

Work was one of the last areas to be affected, but by the 1960s a well-paid, secure job with 'reasonable conditions' was not always enough.[17] Along with the lure of higher wages, jobs were expected to satisfy and to provide meaning and opportunity for creative activity and self-expression. Initially these views were concentrated among the more educated, but by the 1970s many of the less educated aspired to these goals. Psychological, as well as economic, reward was the expectation of work for many people. They felt cheated if they did not find it.

Our samples, like the majority of the adult population in the 1980s, had grown up and been educated and, some of them, experienced much of their adult life under these dominant views and through an historically unique period of twenty years of high employment during the 1950s and 1960s. Whether idealising work as an end in itself or not, men and women had taken for granted that men would need to work for a living and that full-time employment would be available to them. Full employment had become an 'expectable environment'. Most of them had been educated in a system which in 1973 still set out its objectives as self-development and self-realisation of the child and the general adaptation of the student to the world of work.[18] Starting work marked the end of economic dependency and signified a major step into adulthood.

Compared with previous generations, more of them would have gone on to a higher education and expected to acquire professional or skilled status in their anticipated occupation. If their professional sights were high, they would expect to be geographically and socially mobile through their promotions. They would have accepted the dominance of waged or salaried labour, the separation of work from family life, the segmented character of the labour market and their dependence on one form of work. Although Marx wrote about the shift in emphasis from worker as producer to worker as consumer in 1884, many of them will have lived through an acceleration of this change; others will have arrived on this scene, 'the need for money being the real created need of the modern economic system'.[19] The increase of advertising brought forcibly into the home on the television screen whetted appetites as never before.

Although men in full-time employment still outnumber women by more than 2:1, they will have noticed a narrowing in the overall differential and an increasing reliance on two wage earners, varying according to age and numbers of children. The statement, 'Whether a wife works (in *paid employment* [our italics]) is a crucial determinant of whether a family is financially speaking poor'[20] would have meaning for many of them.

In one respect they are different from their forebears of the 1950s and 1960s. Self-provisioning has again increased. With the massive growth of house ownership, the do-it-yourself market has during the 1970s become the fastest growing sector of the building industry. The level of individual productivity has risen in the domestic economy and for many may well be higher than in formal employment. 'It paid me to take a week off work to paint the house.' Yet money is necessary to do this form of work, so, not surprisingly, the employed are the busiest at it. Employment and self-provisioning go together. The most involved in the labour market are also the most involved in using their own labour in their own time for their own purposes.[21] Materials have become cheaper relative to the increasing cost of labour.

The total amount of work has apparently not decreased during the last twenty-five years, but a new divide has occurred; those who are employed often work for longer hours or have two jobs; they sometimes work under more pressure than their forebears and also work at improving their homes; those who are not employed rarely have enough money to be able to work anywhere.

Finally, our 'man of the eighties' knows that his type of employment is the main definer of his and his wife's social status. 'What do you do?' usually means what is your paid employment and is one of the most used opening gambits in establishing a conversation with a stranger in an attempt to 'place' him or her.

The question remains, however, whether the 'expectable environment' of employment under its ideological umbrellas satisfies or, even more, fulfils and, in Maslow's terms, allows the realisation of human needs beyond assured survival. Much of the literature suggests that it does not match the expectations that have been built up about it.

A blessing or a curse?

Work, by its very nature, requires the expenditure of energy and has always, it seems, contained a measure of toil, fatigue, stress and suffering, sometimes compensated by the satisfaction obtained through achievement. However, for many people over long periods of history and in a variety of cultures, employment has been a source of harm, injustice, exploitation, brutalisation and humiliation. An influential minority who own or command the means of production have exploited the larger multitude who lack those means, but share in the process of production. Various accounts of the lives of the factory and mill workers in the nineteenth century suggest that they were treated far worse than the slaves of the ancient Greeks or the mediaeval peasant whose labour was used by the lord of the manor in a system of mutual obligations.

Some forms of work have always been physically dangerous with risk of injury or related illness, and still are. In modern times, conditions and required practice have often not improved with increased knowledge and legally instituted, but not enforced, safeguards.

We have no means of measuring whether modern forms of work are less or more unpleasant than previous ones. Such an assessment depends partly on the worker's expectations and, as we have seen, expectations have risen. Machinery has often intensified, rather than lessened, stress. As a woman weaver wrote in 1924,

> Work inside the factory is much harder than it used to be owing to the great speeding up of the machinery. The toil is now almost ceaseless; the machinery requires constant attention. Thirty years ago this was not the case; the machinery ran very much slower and the operative had a little leisure during working hours ...[22]

Much of the stress of work in pre- or early industrial life would have been directly on the body. Today the stress is also often on the mind, but still shows itself in bodily as well as mental symptoms.

Today the word 'stress' is used much in relation to work by social scientists, psychologists, doctors and managers. Derived from the Latin, the word is not new and the condition is not in itself a bad thing. Bodies and minds were apparently made to withstand some degree of stress and distress. Organs that are not used undergo atrophy. Stress and distress can be a stimulus to growth, achievement and attaining conditions of less stress. It is *too much* stress that can be damaging. Sometimes the word is used as it popularly was in the seventeenth century to emphasise the external stressor – hardship, adversity, poverty. Today many social scientists use the word stress (meaning varying degrees of distress or overstress) and emphasise that it needs to be defined individually, but can only be understood with reference to characteristics of both the individual and the environment and is the outcome of a particular combination of the two.

It has now been well documented that work can be a major cause of too much stress for many people.[23] It has been estimated that stress costs substantially more in terms of lost working days than industrial injury and also more than by strikes. In terms of the interactive concept of the individual and the environment, different types of jobs and work structures occasion different types of stress which will affect some people more than others and, no doubt, this is influential in the types of job people choose, when there is a choice to be exercised. Who can bear the stress and danger of a fire-fighting job when 'A fireman's life is nine years shorter than the average working man because of the beating they take on their lungs and their heart?' Yet the fireman quoted by Terkel in his now famous book, *Working*,[24] preferred that stress to working in a bank. 'You know, it's just paper. It's not real. Nine to five and it's shit. You're looking at numbers. But I can look back and say, "I helped put out a fire. I helped save somebody." It shows something I did on this earth.'

While some jobs demand immense responsibility for other people's lives and property, other jobs demand prolonged periods of concentration. Some people cannot tolerate too much tension in a job, while other people thrive on excitement:

'Actually I enjoy my work when the assignments are large and urgent and somewhat frightening and will come to the attention of many people. I get scared and am unable to sleep at night, but I usually perform my best under this stimulating kind of pressure and enjoy my job the most. I handle all of these important projects myself and I rejoice with tremendous pride and vanity in the compliments I receive when I do them well (as I always do). But between such peaks of challenge and elation there is monotony and despair.'[25]*

A headline in *The Times* in 1986 claimed, 'Illness caused by stress at work "managerial" not medical problem.'[26] The article reported the proceedings of a conference at which it was stated that stress manifested itself in drinking problems or heart disease and was exacerbated by three fundamental occupational dilemmas; too much or too little responsibility; ambiguity of role; and too fierce competition within the organisation for the resources required to achieve the objective. 'These three dilemmas fall within the concept of discrepancy, the gap between a person's ability, training, aptitude, stamina on the one hand, and the demands made on him on the other.' It was noted that while firms are increasingly worried about the effects of stress, few are doing anything constructive about it.

---

* It sounds as if this man needed this excitement to ward off his despair.

Burnout is a phrase that first came into use in 1974,[27] to begin with in relation to human service professions, later in relation to teaching. Writers on this subject distinguish it from temporary fatigue and emphasise that it is not just an event, but a process consisting of three phases.[28] The first phase involves stress from the imbalance between the demands and the resources, both personal and institutional. Feelings of helplessness and hopelessness occur. In the second phase the worker shows a stress reaction in terms of anxiety, tension and exhaustion. The third phase is characterised by a negative adaptation, a psychological withdrawal resulting in apathy, cynicism and rigidity.

For many employed people, the problem is not overload, but underload, too little responsibility, and for those on assembly lines, a dreadful monotony leading to feelings of alienation and diminution of sense of self. Terkel reported that many of his subjects found the automated pace of many jobs wiped out names and faces and, in some instances, feelings.[29] 'I'm just a robot', was said to him time and time again. Individuals told how they had to retreat into fantasies in order to maintain a sense of self while at work. A spot welder who could not move from a two or three foot area all night described the stress for him on the assembly line:

'It didn't stop. It just goes and goes and goes. I bet there's men who have lived and died out there, never seen the end of that line. And they never will – because it's endless. It's like a serpent. It's just all body, no tail. It can do things to you.'

He described how he personally dealt with the stress:

'You get involved with yourself. You dream... I drift back continuously to when I was a kid and what me and my brother did. The things you love most are the things you drift back into. When you dream you reduce the chances of friction with the foreman or the next guy.'

He found his work satisfaction not in his employment, but in his hobby:

'Proud of my work? How can I feel pride in a job where I call a foreman's attention to a mistake... and he'll ignore it. ... So you just go about your work. You have to have pride. So you throw it off to something else. And that's my stamp collection.'

Yet many people regret being forced into retirement at a prescribed age and others, although ready to expend less energy as they approach that age, are aware of the immense adjustment that will be required of them. Younger people, not expecting to be unemployed, are, when they are made so, severely distressed and demoralised. One big question for them is how to spend their still abundant energy. Part of the distress is obviously due to financial insecurity, loss of consumer power, and fear of actual poverty. The spot welder, quoted above, was quite clear that he could find more congenial work, but where, he asked, 'Could I get the money I'm making? Let's face it.' We do not know how much pressure his wife was exerting on him to maintain their achieved standard of living, but, clearly, money with which to buy commodities weighted the scales over his dissatisfaction on the assembly line. What one has can be more important than what one does.

Yet the need to possess this consumer power does not fully explain the drive to work. Work, it seems, means more than that to many people. A British survey[30] of employed people in 1978 found that a majority would not give up work even if they had the opportunity to do so without loss of pay. In a previous American study[31] a similar question was asked and 80% answered that they would keep on working. Two-thirds gave positive reasons; for example, 'working keeps one occupied, gives one an interest'; 'keeps an individual healthy, is good for a person'; 'the kind of work is enjoyable'. Others spoke of the negative results of not working; 'would feel lost if didn't work, would go crazy'; 'wouldn't know what to do with my time, can't be idle'.

A more recent study[32] indicates that motivation to work is declining, but, despite the stress reported in much of the literature – subsequent heart attacks from too much pressure, or alienation from too much boredom – and however much people hate it at times, many of them still seem to want to work and not just for money. Not surprisingly, professional people speak of the satisfaction of use of mind, of exerting influence and holding responsibility. Unskilled workers speak of activity and the use of body as an antidote to boredom or restlessness.[33]

The positive and negative sentiments quoted above are stated more formally by social psychologists studying what have been called the latent functions of work. Marie Jahoda, a social psychologist, writing both in the 1930s and 1970s,[34] explored Freud's proposition that work is man's strongest tie to reality. In explaining why work could be psychologically supportive, even if routine and monotonous, she listed five functions which underlie the manifest function of earning an economic living.

(1) 'Employment imposes a time structure on the waking day.' Many people would agree that exercising self-discipline is no easy task unless highly motivated by reward or recognition. We suspect that now, as in the middle ages, most people have mixed feelings about 'clocking in and out', sometimes resenting it, sometimes welcoming it. In addition, she says that a time-structure ties people to the 'here and now' and 'prevents one from being swamped by the past or dreams of the future'. Yet the spot welder's dreams, apparently not swamping him in his leisure, kept him sane in the work environment.

(2) 'Employment implies regularly shared experiences and contacts with people outside the nuclear family.' This, she says, 'ties one to social reality, enriching knowledge of similarities and differences between individuals ... and providing access to a wider pool of experience than would otherwise be possible.'

(3) 'Employment links an individual to goals and purposes which transcend his own.' This and the previous function indicate the importance of unity and emphasise the social nature of man. We think it is important to emphasise that in institutions there is often an immense gap between the formal ideology and the actual culture on the shop floor. When means of production are often divorced from the visible end product, shared purpose and meaning is often obtained from an underlying culture. As Willis found in his study of a shop floor,

> ...despite bad conditions, despite external direction, despite subjective ravages, people do look for meaning, they do impose frameworks, they do seek enjoyment in activity, they do exercise their abilities. They do, paradoxically, thread through the dread experience of work a living culture, which isn't simply a reflex of defeat. It is a positive transformation of experience and a celebration of shared values in symbols, artefacts and objects.[35]

(4) 'Employment defines aspects of personal status and identity.' Even if status is low and resented on account of that, a defined status may feel better than accordance of none at all.

'Better a robot than a switched off robot', commented one of the members of our workshops.

(5) 'Employment enforces activity.' 'So strong is the need to experience the consequences of one's own deliberate actions, that even those whose jobs are classified as unskilled have been shown to invest considerable ingenuity in varying their performance to demonstrate to themselves what they can do.'

Jahoda points out that other social institutions can offer one or more of these psychological supports, but she knows of none in our society which combines them all and in addition has 'as compelling a manifest reason as making one's living'.

We add to this list a sixth function which has an entirely different dimension and is derived from our psychoanalytic theory: work (including employment) allows for the sublimation (diversion) of primitive impulses into a socially acceptable form. As Menninger has stated, 'of all the methods available for absorbing the aggressive energies of mankind in a useful direction, work takes first place'. It is 'the most practical and obvious of all sublimations'.[36] Freud was not the first person to write about it. As Ovid advised, 'You who seek a termination of your passion, attend to your business; ... soon will voluptuousness turn its back on you.'[37]

Menninger,[38] stressing the diversion of aggression as well as sexuality, emphasises how work represents a fight against something, and an attack upon the environment. In the creative act, much destruction occurs. The farmer, in ploughing his land and tending his crops, tears and pulverises that earth and conducts a steady warfare against weeds and pests which he poisons and kills. We can become quite mournful when we consider the processes to which cotton, for example, is subjected before it appears in the shops – cut, crushed, scorched, torn, boiled, twisted and combed. It is true that the destruction is specialised and selectively directed. 'In work, as contrasted with purposeless destruction, the aggressive impulses are moulded and guided in a constructive direction by the influence of the creative (erotic) instinct.' Drudgery or lack of satisfaction in work, Menninger suggests, occurs when the expression of the aggressive drive is not combined with sufficient eroticism. The worker, quoted on p.29, who peaked on 'challenge and elation' and 'rejoiced with vanity', clearly found a channel for such a combination, as do

many 'strategic' (top level) managers who openly comment on
the exciting thrust of planning and executing change and use a
highly phallic jargon.[39] In contrast, the spot welder found no
such channel, but sought solace in his dreams.

Whereas hard physical work provides for the sublimation of
aggression, different professions, more obviously than unskilled
trades, provide channels of sublimation for a variety of impulses. In addition, the institutional structure and method of work,
often formalised, even ritualised, over many years, provides a
containment for these drives which otherwise might get out of
hand. For example, the greed of a bookie or stockbroker can be
well sublimated and contained as, according to the wisdom of
his advice, he handles, feeds and limits the greed of many of his
customers. As a high financier has said, 'Fear and greed is what
stimulates financial markets – fear that you may lose your
capital and greed if you think somebody is making more.'[40] Jobs
such as these which involve the handling of risk can sublimate a
need or drive for continual excitement or tension.

We want to emphasise the positive aspect of this type of
sublimation and the unconscious wisdom often exercised in
occupational choice when this choice is available. By actively
choosing or finally settling in one type of job which both
highlights and affords containment for what can be problematic
internally, a person is giving himself the chance of maturing
and healing old psychological wounds. We can say it is
healthier, or it is a more lively search for 'daily meaning' to seek
a work environment which highlights one's problem and keeps
it alive for oneself than to avoid what may be a central issue for
the personality. At least it keeps a person in touch with his
problem and, therefore, gives him a chance of solving it. If he
denies himself this chance, he has necessarily less opportunity
to come to terms with it.

We are speaking of unconscious motivation. Consciously
people find a variety of reasons why they choose one career
rather than another. Sometimes they are equally sure that they
prefer one job to another, but are unsure of their reasons.
Whether clearly and consciously formulated or not, this cer-
tainty is indicative of a person with a relatively well formed
self-image and sense of developing adult identity. This sort
of person seems to know who he wants to be and where he
wants to go.

As Carlyle said, 'Blessed is he who has found his work; let him ask no other blessedness.'[41] People whose identity is less well formed may appear to find a job fortuitously: 'I was looking for a job (any job) and took what was available.' If we think in terms of unwritten covenants underlying formal work contracts, we could say this type of person was saying, 'I haven't yet decided who I am and what I want to be. Make of me what you want.' In effect, he is asking the business organisation to substitute for parental authority and to nurture his further growth. If the company fails to nurture and stimulate, this person is likely to become apathetic, working merely for the salary and complaining that no one gives him a break.

Choice of work, made actively or passively – and we emphasise again, *when choice is available* – reveals many aspects of personality and indicates how a person is attempting to form his adult identity. The exercise of that choice means that as well as working for other people's ends, he is also working for himself beyond the economic reward. We believe this is important and, like Willis, are impressed by many people's ability and ingenuity in transforming the experience through sublimation and a variety of symbols to serve their own psychological needs.

Different occupations attract people with a particular underlying motivation which they may well have in common with their colleagues. (This is one factor in the identification with the professional or trade group.) Several studies[42] indicate, for example, that people in the helping professions often had childhoods which were not happy. A study of psychotherapists indicated that they often came from families in which intimacy had got out of hand.[43] Many of them felt they had been enmeshed in their parents' stressful marriage, either having to be a buffer between the parents, or acting as a substitute for one parent in being asked to be too intimate with the other. Left with this problem – a difficulty in handling intimacy – they were attracted to a form of work which both offered intimacy – highly structured transactions of intimacy – yet also offered the opportunity to regulate the stress by the structure of the hourly sessions which they controlled.

Skynner, in an exploration of the themes which emerged in a training programme for marital therapists, also found that many had been attracted to this particular form of therapy because of a problem relating to their parents' marriage.[44] Although a personal handicap of this nature while it remains unconscious may not be helpful to some patients, it promotes empathy and, when made conscious and understood in relation to the self, can be used creatively with a wide range of patients.

Abse, considering the relationship between personality and the choice of career in respect of politicians, considered they were unusually endowed with aggression which they sublimate into the clever use of words and oratory.[45] He suggested that in order to master their aggression, they need to talk incessantly. The House of Commons clearly provides a strong containment of this need to talk. Pointed questions to the adversary of the other Party have to be put through a third person – the Speaker. The adversary is safe on the other side of the debating chamber, an actual line firmly keeping the two sides apart to prevent the use of fists. Using a Freudian explanation of their behaviour, he presumes that most MPs would not want to have their choice of occupation put in anal terms – 'The impress of the anal phase of development ... accompanied by aggressive fantasies ... is deeply imprinted upon his character.' Yet the fact remains, he says, that they choose to take their seats for a large part of the year in a Chamber where they continue to pass motions!

Evans[46] explored the motivation underlying choice of a foreign language as a subject of study and further career by students and staff in a university. He found that for many of them the choice was significant in the formation of their identity. Oppressed by their own family or the wider culture of their upbringing, they had difficulty in establishing their own sense of difference or separateness. As one of his subjects said:

> 'English, my mother tongue, was slightly contaminated by the emotional input of my family. So there were lots of phrases and lots of expressions that used to make me anxious. When I discovered another language ... I could learn these idioms ... and the use of them was in some ways delightful, new and not emotionally laden.'

Another said, 'I wanted to be removed from my family, my society, my culture, my language ...'. As Evans says, 'to opt for a foreign culture is to opt against an English one'. Many of his subjects had found strong emotional bonds with the culture of the language they had chosen either in childhood or in their compulsory year in that country while studying for their degree. They gave accounts of 'fun' and 'happiness' and of letting themselves be embraced by the sun and the ample bosoms of landladies. We suggest that they were able to allow themselves this experience of 'more open, more loving' families, just because their foreignness in that country still reminded them of difference and mitigated the fear of being swamped and taken over.

Pruyser[47] also illustrates the use of a job which particularly heightens and exemplifies an inherent conflict. He describes how a Minister of the Church works for a salary which is conspicuously low for the number of years spent in higher education. The dissatisfaction that may be felt about this is, he suggests, mitigated by the individual's satisfaction derived from his identification with the 'suffering servant'. The ambition to be a competent professional may be held in tense opposition to the altogether different motive of being a humble respondent to a divine call.

Dependence/dominance (or authority/obedience) are facts of life and inherent in many jobs and life situations. This conflict is highlighted in the work of a priest. If he can come to terms with the problem in the external world, he serves his inner world and finds satisfaction in what was previously felt to be so unsatisfactory.

From much of what we have written in this section, it is clear that job satisfaction/dissatisfaction has many aspects and is highly complex. A job can dissatisfy at one level and satisfy at another, both levels fully conscious. Many people have mixed feelings about their jobs, liking this, disliking that about it. A job can also dissatisfy at a conscious level and satisfy at an unconscious one. As has been said, 'We pay with conscious pain for unconscious satisfaction.' And what can be or become fully conscious for one person, like the linguist who was more anxious in her mother tongue than in a foreign language, can be quite unconscious for another, perhaps less introspective person.

When jobs are relatively freely available, major dissatisfaction with a job by a person who continues to remain in it, often says as much about the person as the job itself. Why for instance, does the high fashion model, quoted by Terkel,[48] complain that 'she is just an object'? Even when jobs are not so easy to come by, it is equally not easy to become a high fashion model. Why does she choose to be treated as an object? In fact she can get immense recognition, some sort of prestige, and, if at the top of her class, is well recompensed, thereby satisfying several levels of needs in Maslow's hierarchy. It seems that she easily identifies with being an object, but her complaint suggests that other needs inside her are asking for some expression. Apparently she is afraid of forsaking the achieved satisfaction, but has not enough conviction that she can be more than someone else's object and thereby achieve a higher level of satisfaction.

As Menzies[49] has demonstrated in her classic study of nursing, the defensive system of an individual must be roughly consistent with the group defensive system established in an organisation for satisfaction to outweigh dissatisfaction in the employee. Nursing in some hospitals is renowned for the depersonalisation of the patient – 'the liver in bed 10' – used as a group defence against the stress of the job and the pain and suffering to which a nurse is exposed. Nurses who will not put up with the depersonalisation of the patient (who do not need to use that defence) either find another job in a hospital which does not adopt this defensive culture, move into private nursing or community services, or they leave the profession altogether. They also leave or do not consider going into the profession if they do not have their own idiosyncratic need to care for other people in an environment in which the dependency of the patient is so exemplified.

As Lawrence[50] has said, 'The individual can be understood as living in a "double environment"': the external environment as it is and as the individual perceives it; and the internal environment of the individual which has been formed over the years by a variety of experiences, some remembered, some not, and by a whole collage of images, fantasies, fears and conflicts, many of which have been repressed. The latter affects the perception of the former, but the two need to be relatively compatible for there to be, in Willis' terms, a transformation by which the individual makes the external world his own to suit his purpose. When, as we stated in the Introduction, the outer world (environment) confirms the best of inner fantasies and images, people feel they are recreating and confirming what is good in themselves. When the external environment is more benign than the existing internal one, old ghosts can be, if not entirely laid to rest, at least appeased and kept in hand.

We have been impressed by how many people in our sample had tried to use their previous jobs to lay old ghosts. It was in starting to work with them when they had been made redundant, that we found we needed to learn what they had sublimated or symbolised in their job which could no longer find expression when they were out of work. Whatever the mixture of the dissatisfaction/satisfaction equation – their ambivalence about the job – they were often 'shattered' by the loss of it. Their experience of loss seemed beyond what can be understood or explained in terms of the poverty that often goes hand in hand with unemployment.

Some had achieved a successful transformation of the work environment. Others, although having found themselves a work environment which had potential for mediation by highlighting the personality problem, had not done so well, often because of the degree of conflict inherent in their problem. We detail some of the idiosyncratic ways that some people in our samples had used, sometimes successfully, in transforming their work experience.

Old ghosts

Sublimation: Mr Kettlewell's sadism

Mr Kettlewell sought and found an obvious sublimation and containment for his violent and sadistic impulses in his employment. For many years he was a prison officer. Large, robust and superficially jovial, he made few friends. It seemed he was feared rather than respected and liked. 'Driven', as if perpetually frightened of the consequences if he did not exert enough control, he was always the first to opt for extra duties. He worked, he worked and he worked. Finally the containment provided by the nature of the job was not enough; his impulses got the better of him and his services were no longer required.

He had had a desperately sad childhood, but could not allow himself to know about his fury. When encouraged to think more about what had happened to him, he could only nod his

head and mumble, 'They [his parents] did their best.' Without
a job he remained a defeated man, unable to talk about
himself, his despair and shame; his feelings were only
apparent in his slumped body. His spirits revived and his
physical symptoms disappeared when he obtained work as a
bailiff; executing writs, he regained his composure.

Sublimation: Mr Treacher's fear of chaos

Mr Treacher also needed to keep things in control, but found a
more creative way of doing it. He was an apron manager and
thought his job was 'fantastic'. He did a 'proper' job, parking
aeroplanes on the airport apron; 'if a plane was two or three
feet out of position', it could 'snarl up the whole airport –
there's no two ways about it'. He and his mate, Bob, with whom
he always worked the shift, patrolled conscientiously and
parked immaculately. In describing this activity, he drew a
map of the airport to illustrate the complexity. He and Bob
despised the younger apron managers who, he said, 'sat
through the night with cans of beer'. Apparently, Mr Treacher
and Bob were equally despised by these other managers who
refused to work with them and, we can imagine, sniggered at
their pedantic ways.

Mr Treacher had a need for order and predictability which
kept an inner chaos at bay. This need for precise order was met
for him in the actual task he was expected to perform. There
was a congruence between the expectations of the outer world
and the internal needs of Mr Treacher. In addition, he had a
congenial workmate, apparently with the same need for
orderly precision, who was as obsessional and dependable as
he. Further, he had a boss who respected their methods of
plane parking and did not interfere. This was of particular
importance to Mr Treacher. When he was a child, he had felt
'rubbished' by his father who rarely allowed him to do anything
for himself. When he tried, his father usually said, 'That's a
load of rubbish. You're not doing it properly. Let me do it.' His
boss never 'rubbished' him nor contradicted his immaculate
plans.

In this job Mr Treacher did not lay the 'rubbish' ghost to final
rest. It must still have lurked in the background. It reared its
head again when Mr Treacher acquired a new boss, a much

younger man who contradicted his and Bob's parking plans. Mr Treacher again felt 'rubbished'. In his eyes, the new boss's decisions were often wrong; muddle, which Mr Treacher's ghost magnified into chaos, ensued. The new boss never admitted he had made a mistake. There was the same sadness in Mr Treacher's voice when he described this as when he spoke of his father. Low in spirits, he visited his GP regularly over the next eighteen months with depressive symptoms.

Father's love: Mr Holloway's symbol

Many of the husbands in our samples had found means of dealing with deep feelings about their fathers through their employment. For example, Mr Holloway's job enabled him to preserve a good image of his father who had been largely absent in his childhood, repeatedly deserting the family and finally leaving for good. When Mr Holloway was seventeen, his father briefly reappeared and found him an apprenticeship. A few years later his father died. Mr Holloway exercised a skill, earned good money and got on well with his workmates. He gained satisfaction at many levels, but, above all, this particular job remained the symbol of his father's love for him.

The danger of conflict: Mr Salmon's conformity

Mr Salmon had a less obvious problem in relation to his father, but brought up in a family in which no difference or conflict could be expressed, he could not withstand his father's urging him to be a policeman. His father was in an unskilled job and highly ambitious for his son to realise what he had not been able to do. Mr Salmon did not just have to 'better himself', but also to do a job which exemplified control for a father who could not tolerate conflict.

Having talked to a random group of Police cadets, James[51] reported:

> They have all enrolled for the expected reasons: pay, security, a job worth doing. Beyond that they positively gleam with motivation. ... They have absolutely no illusions about the moral problems that face them. 'It is going to be "us and

them". .... But if they give us a fair chance we can crack it,' says one.

Mr Salmon senior urged his son to take a job which would take care of his own problem. However, because of the model portrayed to him throughout his childhood, Mr Salmon himself needed to sort out something about the danger of conflict. By this time he had his own internal problem as well as having to carry his father's: should he confirm his father's love by doing what he wanted, or should he try to live his own life and promote his own identity and meaning?

At first the externalisation of conflict served him quite well. Although, as we might guess, overstressed by the degree of conflict to which he was exposed in this job, he witnessed and helped to contain much conflict, and obtained vicarious satisfaction from the anti-social (anti-familial) impulses which he could not express himself. He also obtained immense satisfaction from his father's pride (love) in him.

However, during the miners' strike of 1984/85, Mr Salmon had to do his stint on the picket lines. The degree of conflict was too much for him and the strike, extending over so many months, was apparently unresolvable. It stressed him beyond his toleration. As he said, he could not bear the sight and knowledge of a 'divided town', symbolising as this apparently did for him a divided family.

By this time Mr Salmon's father had died. Mr Salmon was clear that his father's death was one factor in his leaving the force. He was also clear that, quite apart from finding the job too stressful, he wanted to establish his own identity. Yet he remained conflicted. One part of him still wanted to identify with his father; another part of him felt a failure because he had not realised his father's aspiration.

It was unfortunate for Mr Salmon that in attempting to deal with his own and his father's internal problem of 'them and us' (father/son), the expectable environment symbolised conflict in such an extreme form. No doubt, in any job he would have displayed a problem in dealing with conflict in a mature way. If, however, he had not been so driven to realise his father's ambition and needs, he might have got himself into an environment in which lesser forms of conflict, more easily solved, would have mitigated his fears.

Confusion: Mr Collins' defiance

In contrast, Mr Collins' choice of occupation, that of jazz musician, was partly an act of defiance against his father's detailed plans for him to be a lawyer. His lack of success and of application in this job combined with unrealistic expectations of himself suggested that he was as conflicted as Mr Salmon. On the one hand he had to be different and defy; on the other, he was frightened of being successful, or even reasonably so. In addition, his upbringing had left him confused as to the value of diligence. His father had prospered, but only after a long, hard struggle. He indulged his son, wanting to make life easier for him than it had been for himself. At the same time he was envious of his son for having 'had it made' for him. He was both indulgent and critical.

At a conscious level, Mr Collins became increasingly dissatisfied with his work and his own lack of application. Unlike Mr Treacher, he did not find a father-substitute who would value his efforts and talent in a less conflicted way than his father had done. His work did not help him to repair. However, it gave him some satisfaction. Like Mr Holloway, it kept him in touch with a deceased parent. His mother, also much absent in his childhood, through her pursuit of the Arts, had died when he was adolescent. Unsure of her love for him, in comparison with her love for the Arts, he partly tried to please her in an identification by trying to pursue an artistic career, but at the same time he expressed his anger with her and his father in a passive, self-destructive lack of application.

Mr Collins failed to mitigate his complex internal conflict about both his indulging, depriving and confusing parents. In his choice of occupation he kept the conflict alive in himself and, therefore, in our terms, was still struggling with the problem of his own life and meaning, although failing to resolve it. He could have been economically better off and psychologically worse off if he had taken a job safer in economic and psychological terms – a job not exemplifying the problem for him. Even in his failure, he was keeping himself in touch with his own problem and, therefore, still with some hope that he might sometime be able to do something about it. He needed therapy to do this in order to make a more realistic decision as to whether to allow himself to succeed in this or another profession.

Compensation: Mr Appleby's new perspective

Mr Appleby had derived no expectation of work satisfaction from his melancholic father. Over many years he had 'got by' in several jobs and then had a prolonged period of unemployment. Eventually he obtained work as a driver for a Social Services Day Centre, a job of lower status than those he had done before. However, this job motivated and satisfied him in a way no previous one had done. He explained his satisfaction on two counts. First, he could identify with his passengers, so he wanted to help them with his kindness and cheerfulness in a way that he would have liked to have been helped by his father. He found he was appreciated, although, as he carefully explained, he did not attempt to do what the social workers did. Second, some of the sad situations of his passengers put his own continuing difficulties in perspective. It was a relief to know that he was not as badly off as they were.

Masculinity: Mr Skelton's fear of puniness

Mr Skelton's job helped him to mitigate a basic fear. He was in regular employment for most of his working life as a builder's labourer – on *heavy* work, he emphasised. He found pride and meaning in his strength which enabled him to do this type of work. He had been much affected by the insecurity of his father's work as a farm labourer during the 1930s depression. When Mr Skelton senior was put off work, he had to join the itinerant labour force and offer himself for hire at the annual mop fair, a corn dolly in his lapel to indicate his availability. Keeping fit had been of major significance to the family in which there were nine children; the obviously big, strong and healthy men were the first to be hired.

Quite apart from the size of the family and the problem of so many mouths to feed, we can imagine the amount of anxiety generated as hiring time came round. We do not know if Mr Skelton senior was large or puny; whether Mr Skelton was proud of his big, strong Dad for getting hired first, or bitterly ashamed and worried when a puny Dad got hired last or not at all. We suspect it might be the latter, as Mr Skelton quickly became a psychological shadow of his former self when after an accident at work he was not able to continue with heavy labouring. Alternative, indoor, lighter work he dismissed as 'women's work'. In addition, his son, a notably puny lad, was soon in trouble, committing a series of offences. Puniness was evidently a problem for this boy and for his father who, while complaining about his son's behaviour in and outside the home, clearly had much sympathy for him and seemed to obtain gratuitous pleasure from his anti-social, at times physically aggressive behaviour.

A job which overtly defined adult masculinity was clearly important for many men in our sample. When redundant and unable to find similar work, when unsupported in their masculinity in a strong, male group, they had difficulty in continuing to 'feel a man'. It was as if, like Mr Treacher and Mr Collins, no innate confidence had been built up in childhood. Some had been kept a 'Mummy's boy'.

Mothers: Mr Bell's failure to grow up

Mr Bell described himself as a mother's boy and managed to get himself mothered in his job in a way which did not help him to grow up but just fed and over stimulated his narcissism. He had not been able to identify with his drunken father who had taken scant interest in him. His happier memories were associated only with his mother who encouraged his musical ability. He had no problem in finding work with a successful band. The manager looked after all his needs, both basic and quite luxurious. When informed of the next run of engagements and provided with a plane ticket all he had to do was to get himself to the airport. When he flew from one major city to another in Europe and in the Americas, he was shepherded into coach or taxi, fed and bedded down with 'even girls laid on'. With all things arranged, apparently not needing to extend himself beyond his ready competence with his instrument, satisfied by the nightly applause, he remained emotionally like a young boy. For many years he was satisfied with this way of life.

Maturation: Mr Todd's escape from mother

Mr Todd was also a mother's boy. He had a congenital speech defect severe enough for it to be difficult for other people to understand him until they got used to the distorted sounds he produced. This defect seriously impaired his relationships and confidence in himself as a child. Not surprisingly he was excessively shy. In addition his mother, a bossy woman, had grossly over-protected him and kept him tied to her apron strings. As a young adult he did not have the confidence to leave home nor to enter the courting scene.

Slowly, however, through his job as a short-distance lorry driver and loader for a relatively small firm with a stable workforce, he started to feel better about himself. He was with this firm for sixteen years. His work was valued and in return he offered his loyalty. His job offered him a self-definition which he had failed to acquire under his mother's wing. For many years, still unable to leave home, at least at work he was a man. His mates learned to understand him and he became a regular frequenter of the works' small social club. Through this club he acquired a wife who was strong enough to wean him from his mother's clutches.

Underlying need: Mr Ryan's new family

Whereas Mr Todd found a masculine group which promoted his manhood in a way his family failed to do, Mr Ryan found a much needed extended family in his job as a farm worker in a tied cottage. In contrast to what he had experienced as a child in an unpredictable family, 'dragged up' by his older sisters, he came to feel a valued person on the farm and in the tight-knit rural community.

Mr Todd, partly on account of his disability, had been kept too dependent on his mother. Mr Ryan had been forced too early into a premature independency, leaving him very insecure underneath his apparent ability to get by. For opposing reasons, both of them had what we would term strong 'dependency needs'. They settled in jobs, Mr Todd for sixteen years, Mr Ryan for eleven years, in which some of these needs were met. Along with the financial security, they found an underlying emotional security which enabled them to respond to the demands made upon them, to grow up, find wives and to prove themselves to be more effective husbands and fathers than their own fathers had been. They seemed well set for life.

Within the expectable environment of employment, most (49) men in our samples had been in regular work and had economically sustained themselves and their families. They had exercised a variety of skills, sometimes only modest. They had found companionship and linked themselves to purposes beyond their own. In addition, they had found, at least containment for their underlying fears and problems, sometimes creatively so, and at best, symbolic meaning in making a living. This idiosyncratic personal symbolism by which they 'transformed' their jobs related back to experiences in childhood.

The reader may be surprised that the old ghosts we have described have all been those of the husbands, not those of the wives. Being wise after the event, we now wish we had enquired more about the paid employment of the wives who were working outside the home (50%). However, except in one case, it was the husband's unemployment which brought a couple into the samples. The loss of their jobs was what they chose to speak about and then, only with our encouragement, about what these jobs meant to them. In no case did the employment of the wife take precedence over that of her husband. Her job accommodated his job and her domestic and child care concerns. In the next chapter on love and marriage we come back to this relationship between the women's paid work outside the home and unpaid work in the home.

3
Making a Loving

Jack saw the other men at the beginning of the working day ...
and also at the end when they came home. On winter mornings,
when it was still dark, he didn't recognise them unless they
stood close to him in the queue ... The fact of going to work hid
the separate identity; it was hard to imagine that each man,
lying in bed with his wife half an hour before, had been someone
unique and private.

Mervyn Jones

Man's love is of man's life a thing apart,
Tis woman's whole existence.

Byron

In this chapter we look at another main sphere of life – another
expectable environment – in which people seek to repair and
improve what was felt to be wrong in the past and in doing so
find purpose and meaning in their lives.

Just as man has had to work from the beginning of time to
sustain himself, so he has paired and apparently plighted his
troth either informally under the hawthorn tree or more
formally with witnesses in a marriage ceremony.

In terms of the possibility for him of sexual gratification all
the year round (unlike animals, independent of oestrus), the
innate potential ability to form intimate, affectionate alliances,
the time it takes to rear the human child, and the protected
environment required for mother and children, it is not hard to
understand why a contracted relationship between a man and
a woman has been so persistent throughout history and defied
ideological attempts to dismantle both it and discrete family
formation within, for example, Kibbutzim or other types of
communes.

It seems that family formation with a view to permanency is
a universal characteristic of mankind, an expression of

biological and archetypal functioning only secondarily modified by cultural or ecological features. As the anthropologist Fox has stated:

> The apparently endless kinds of kinship and marriage arrangements known to men are in fact variations on a few themes ... Once one gets behind the surface manifestations, the uniformity of human behaviour and of human social arrangements is remarkable.[1]

Theoretically we extend Bowlby's theory of attachment,[2] which he believes has a biological basis, to explain the consistent drive of men and women to pair and bond. He defines attachment behaviour as 'seeking and maintaining proximity to another individual' for the purpose of safety. Describing the attachment behaviour of young animals and children, he notes two main characteristics of this behaviour. The first is proximity and the use of a safe attachment figure as a base from which to explore the world and to which to retreat in times of need. The need may be internal – hunger, sickness or fatigue – or it may be occasioned by threat of external danger or of loss of the attachment figure. When danger threatens or need of succour or comfort makes itself felt, heightened attachment behaviour can be observed. The second characteristic is specificity; an alternative figure does not suffice.

In animals this behaviour is apparent from birth, the ewe and its own lamb recognising each other and both of them distressed if they cannot find each other. In humans the system is only incipient in the first few months of life, but becomes much more manifest in the second half year and remains so until the third or fourth year. According to the trust that is developed in help being available when required, attachment behaviour remains at a fairly low level throughout life, but is heightened in times of need such as illness, the birth of a child or old age. Adolescents, in seeking their adult autonomy, often display extreme swings of behaviour between fierce independence and clinging proximity.

Marriage or committed adult partnership provides the opportunity for re-attachment to a specific figure.[3] It denotes a settling down. Like starting work it symbolises a step into adulthood. (The majority of young people in Britain today only leave the home of their parents when they marry and with their new spouse set up a home of their own.[4] At the same time marriage can provide a safe base and an emotional container. Just as a young child needs to be contained and given safety and security as a base from which to explore and develop mastery of skills and to which to retreat when his efforts fail, so too can an adult develop more of his own fullness of nature if he provides himself with an attachment figure on whom he can rely.

There is disagreement as to how long the single marriage family (the nuclear family, as it is called), contrasted with an extended family, has existed in this country as the primary household unit. Some historians and anthropologists have claimed, as in Leach's words, that 'it is a most unusual kind of organisation and I predict that it is only a transient phase in our society'.[5]

However, the historian, Macfarlane, argues that 'the English now have roughly the same family system as they had in 1250'.[6] Similarly, Houlbrooke, writing of the English family between 1450 and 1700, states, 'Six hundred years ago the nuclear family was the basic element of human society, as it still is today ... the commonest type of residential unit'.[7] Even then, strong conjugal and parental affection existed as ideals and in practice. Kinship ties were relatively weak with no sense of exclusive or over-riding loyalty or obligation to support. As only one part of the social network system, some relatives were loved in their own right, others were used for advancement, or hospitality, or as contacts, or intermediaries, and yet others were held at arm's length or the relationship soured by legal disputes over inheritance or property rights. Macfarlane, commenting on the diary of Ralph Josselin, a seventeenth-century clergyman, said how 'startled' he was to find

... how 'modern' his world was; his family life, attitudes to children, economic anxieties, and the very structure of his thought was very familiar indeed. ... His feelings were instantly recognisable. Of course there were features that were different; a constant background of chronic sickness, a marked interest in the Day of Judgement, certain political and religious beliefs. Yet it was his similarity rather than the difference which was striking.[8]

As the sociologist, Bernard, points out, 'There is something timeless running through the accounts of specific husbands and wives from the past and from the present, a thread of human continuity which runs through all the institutional diversity.'[9]

Institutional diversity

Despite this thread of continuity, economic and social factors have strongly influenced marriage over the centuries – its occurrence, its timing, the amount of control exerted by the Church or State, and the roles performed within it.

In some periods of history lack of work and the accompanying poverty have delayed or even prohibited marriage. Contemporary accounts of a series of courtships or prolonged courtship in the middle ages suggest that age of marriage was partially determined by the ability to support a family, and commentators on the social scene saw young marriages as a cause of 'social ills'.[10] Wages and marriage rates fell sharply during the late sixteenth century, the marriage rate reviving between 1556 and 1581 in response to a short-lived rise in wages. After the continuing bad harvests in the late 1580s the Poor Law overseers prohibited men from entering their parish if they intended to marry.[11] Clergymen supported these restrictions by refusing to marry these potential immigrants.

Spinsterhood has rarely been enviable; as described in many novels, the lot of the governess or aunt – the 'old maid' – in the seventeenth or eighteenth centuries was quite intolerable and to be avoided if at all possible. In modern Britain, 'the avenue to success' in social and economic terms for the girl from a working-class home is still more likely to be through marriage and her husband's earning capacity than her own.[12] Women still tend to be less qualified[13] and less well paid at work than men. Further, the availability of living accommodation affects the timing of marriage.[14] Today there is little accommodation to be rented cheaply. Many young couples expect to own their house, but despite the ease of obtaining large mortgages, the outlay is considerable. This may delay the marriage and will require, at least for a period, most young wives to continue earning.

Health factors and morbidity rates have at times combined with economic situations to affect both ease of marriage and likelihood of remarriage. After the Black Death in 1384 land became more available than it had been and the age of marriage fell.[15] Over the last and present centuries public health measures and advances in medical practice have left their influence. Lowered infant and adult mortality rates have prolonged life and, therefore, the length of many marriages. (Between 1901 and 1983 average life expectancy at birth increased from 48 to 71 years for men and from 51 to 77 for women.[16]) This has had immense implications for the staying power of the partners. The readier availability of more reliable forms of contraception than used previously has enabled women to delay parenthood and reduce the size of the average family and the span of childbearing and rearing years, thus freeing married women for the labour market outside the home. (From 1946 to the mid-1980s the proportion of married women in the labour market has more than doubled. In the same period fertility has fallen below the replacement level.[17])

In Britain, as in other western countries, marriage has been increasingly controlled first by the Church, and then by the State. However, only gradually did the Church raise marriage from a civil contract to a religious sacrament, to be ratified in public and subject to ecclesiastical as well as common law with many prohibited degrees of affinity. Even in the middle ages many marriages were still contracted privately, 'with the ecclesiastical courts desperately trying to regulate, register and make indissoluble these "private marriages"'.[18] The problem facing the Courts concerning matrimonial or betrothal disputes was whether the contract made 'in a blacksmith's shop, near a hedge, in a kitchen, by an oak tree, even on the King's highway' had been, 'I take you as my wife now' or 'I promise to marry you sometime in the future'.[19] The 1753 Marriage Act legislated that all marriages had to be solemnised by a clergyman, recorded in the parish register and that no marriage under the age of 21 was valid without consent of parent or guardian. Children of informal long-term unions were for the first time deemed to be bastards.

The Church gradually eroded the right to divorce which in Anglo-Saxon times could be achieved either by mutual consent or the will of one party. The ecclesiastical courts granted annulments on the grounds of a previous contract made with another person, and separation orders on the grounds of adultery, cruelty or continual quarrels. The poorer members of society simply divorced themselves by running away, a recourse more open to men than to women. In the sixteenth and seventeenth centuries, as now, deserted wives and children formed a sizeable proportion of the poor. Second marriages after official separations needed to be authorised by Act of Parliament, but unauthorised second marriages were said to be common. Divorce was first formalised by Act of Parliament in 1698.

Church and State have also regulated the balance of power within marriage and after divorce. The Church's teaching of Saint Paul's doctrine of wifely submission was reinforced by the economic and social situation of women when they became dependent on their husband's waged labour and relegated to the domestic hearth. The wife's foremost duty was obedience: 'Wives be in subjection unto your husband ... for the husband is the head of the wife, as Christ also is the head of the Church.'[20] However, this teaching was mitigated by emphasis on the husband's duty to treat his wife with tender consideration and respect.[21] Yet at the same time the Church reinforced the 'double standard' maintained in a basically patriarchal society in which common law underpinned the husband's power and authority; for example, the ecclesiastical courts considered adultery to be a more serious offence for a wife than a husband.[22]

In 1857 the State set up a special matrimonial court to replace the ecclesiastical one, but as marriage became more and more regulated through legislation, married women ceased to have legal existence. 'It was almost impossible for men to divorce their wives and absolutely impossible for women to divorce their husbands.'[23] Everything she previously owned belonged to her husband, even her children. His rights as a father were absolute. It was not until 1923 than women could obtain divorce on the same grounds as men and not until 1973 that a married woman achieved equal legal authority over her children.

Roles within marriage and the amount of separation or togetherness has altered over the centuries. In the middle ages the growth of civil peace meant that less often than previously were wives left in charge of estate or holding. Later, easier transport enabled wives to travel with their husbands. As they came to spend more time together, what were often complementary roles became more integrated, only to become less so when, as we noted in the last chapter, work became concentrated in mills and factories, and following the Factory Acts the husband became isolated from his wife and children for many hours each day.

The last twenty-five years

In modern Britain there has been no marked change in the total number of marriages between 1961 (397,000) and 1985 (393,000).[24] However, there has been a steady decrease in the number of first marriages and a steady increase in the number of second and subsequent marriages – 35% of all marriages. The decline in first marriages is due to several factors: a reflection of the eligible population following a declining birth rate since 1961; a trend towards later marriage, the number of teenage marriages declining; and an increased prevalence of cohabitation before marriage. The increase in second and third marriages is due to the greater ease of getting out of an unsatisfactory marriage following the Divorce Reform Act of 1969 which introduced a solitary reason for divorce – 'the irretrievable breakdown of marriage' – and the Matrimonial Proceedings Act of 1984 which allowed people to petition for divorce after one year, instead of three years, of marriage. In 1985, 175,000 decrees were made absolute, more than double the number in 1971.

Because of the ready availability of divorce, an increase in the illegitimacy rate and a decrease in the number of illegitimate children placed for adoption, the number of one-parent households has increased. Yet, because of the remarriage rate, the number of households headed by a married couple has fallen only slightly in these years and still stands at just over three-quarters of all private households.[25] It seems that the urge to marry or, when a marriage fails, to find another 'better' partner remains a driving force in our society.

Within this statistical context, women seem less pleased with their marriage than their husbands do compared with some 25 years earlier. Although which partner applies for a divorce may not always be a true reflection of the actual state of affairs, women now petition for divorce in far greater numbers than men.*[26] This dissatisfaction follows some emancipation of women, a gaining of some legal equalities, regaining of rights previously lost, an increase in the number of married women working full time (20%) and part time (24%), and, as mentioned in the last chapter, an 'age of psychology' in which values of self realisation are promoted.

In 1971 Gorer compared the results of two surveys undertaken in 1950 and 1969.[27] In 1950 many couples stressed the importance of being efficient in their roles as breadwinners or housewives. In 1969 the emphasis was on comradeship and doing things together:

> Today this is mentioned by nearly a third of all our respondents, compared with barely half that number twenty years ago.
>
> ...
>
> In 1950 ... husbands and wives put a lot of emphasis on moral and economic qualities; ... in 1969 the emphasis had been shifted to psychological qualities; understanding, love and affection, patience, equanimity, shared responsibilities and interests.

In line with liberal and progressive social aspiration for equal opportunities for men and women, and following the progressive force of the women's liberation movement and the 1975 Sexual Discrimination Act, there is a widely held view among professional couples that marriage, with an emphasis on comradeship and togetherness, is a union of equals. The idea is extended to a belief that work in the home – domestic and child care – should be shared when the wife, like the husband, is employed outside the home. In the last 35 years there has been an enormous growth in the number of employed married women.†[28] However, recent research,[29] although confirming the ideology of egality, indicates that action, or lack

* In 1961, 18,000 women and 14,000 men petitioned; in 1985, 139,000 women and 52,000 men petitioned. In 1985, 72% of divorces were granted to women.
† 1931, 10%   1971, 42%
  1951, 22%   1985, 52%

of action, belies the words. There is little evidence of husbands taking their full share of domestic or child care tasks. As Halsey has stated:

> There are no firm statistics concerning the involvement of men in the domestic economy. What we do know ... is that clearly tradition is persistent: women still bear the main burden of domestic management in practice, and equal sharing is more of an ideal than a reality and honoured by men more in the breach than in the observance.[30]

The husband's job is more often than not given priority and many brides change their job on marriage. If they return to work after a birth or when all the children have reached school age, 37% do so lower down the occupational scale.[31] Much of this downward mobility is associated with the need to combine part-time work with domestic responsibilities. For many women, marriage is work and, even if not consuming most of their time, remains their first priority. Convenient hours are vital to them and part-time employment tends to be more available in less skilled occupations.

Priority given to the husband's employment with the wife's employment fitting round domestic commitments means that many women are married to their husbands' careers. As Finch has written:

> In so far as the majority of women still take on the major responsibility for feeding and clothing a man and caring for his children, they present men's employers with workers who are good employees, that is people who have unbroken work records, who do not have regular periods of absence and are also available to work a pattern of hours suitable to the employers. In other words, women present employers with men who are fit for work and freed for work, and employers are enabled to organise their operations in a way which assumes that men do not have commitments to children, to elderly relatives or indeed to caring for themselves.[32]

As Mansfield has stated, marriage may be 'more equal perhaps – but not equal'. She continues:

> We must be careful to check the pervasiveness of the ideology of egalitarian marriage. This is how dreams become expectations. And dreams are rarely fulfilled.[33]

Expectations must to some extent determine satisfaction or dissatisfaction. Throughout the ages expectations have often been higher than the reality – higher than many historians have previously believed. And marital disharmony, according to observers in different centuries, has always been widespread and attributed to severe living and economic conditions which placed unbearable strain on the partners,* failure in mutual adjustment, personality problems of one or both partners, marrying too young,† and rash and impulsive choice of partner.

Choice of partner

Choice of partner, like freedom to marry or not to marry, has always, it seems, been curtailed to some extent by economic and social circumstances and pressures: the balance or imbalance of the sexes and availability of suitable partners; the drive to better oneself, for example by the apprentice's marrying the master's daughter; the prospect of employment and ability to sustain a family; (in the early 1980s the social life of young unemployed men has limited their opportunity for meeting potential partners and has diminished their eligibility in the eyes of the women).[36]

In feudal times, the economic consideration was that of the lord of the manor who had a vested interest in the 'in marriage' of his serfs, since an 'out marriage' deprived him of labour. The disobedient who did not seek permission could be fined.[37] Not surprisingly, parents have usually held strong views as to the suitability of a prospective partner for their offspring, the wisdom of the older generation forecasting the unhappy outcome of what is seen to be a foolish marriage. The degree to which their views have influenced the young to the extent of arranging, encouraging or discouraging (subtly or otherwise) a liaison has shown most variation between different social classes. In mediaeval times, marriages arranged by parents, relatives or benefactors were more common in the propertied

---

* In 1979 divorce rates were four times higher in Social Class V than in Social Class I.[34]

† In 1979, 'spouses who marry in their teens are almost twice as likely to divorce as those who marry between the ages of 20 and 24'.[35]

classes, particularly for the eldest children. Marriages could create powerful alliances, recover and enlarge property and amass wealth.[38] In the middle ranks of society in the seventeenth century young people had a wider choice of partner, but if the parental views were ignored, the young couple could suffer:

> The parents on both sides were displeased, (or seemed soe) with this match, and therefore allowed the new marryed couple noe maintenance.[39]

However, until the twentieth century many parents were not alive by the time their children were of marrying age or could not provide for them if they were. The young working-class citizens were mainly dependent on their own resources. They met their future spouse in the ale house, at the dance, or when in service or apprenticeship often some way from home.[40]

It has been argued that romantic love is a relatively modern phenomenon, in earlier times only the business of troubadours and illicitly of the rich. We do not know much about the feelings of the poorer sections of society. Unable to write, they did not record them. The more literate classes were apparently uninterested in the personal lives of serfs, servants and tradesmen. Yet the records of fines for disobedience in the matter of choice of spouse and the use of love potions[41] suggests that they experienced loving feelings in respect of one person rather than another, just as we do today. As Colman suggests, the silence 'signifies exactly the same as the silence of a company's annual report on the personal lives of its employees: lack of interest. No one would conclude from company reports that workers had no personal relations, and no one should conclude from the silence of manorial rolls that serfs had no personal relations.'[42]

Literature suggests that prior love has long been deemed to be compatible with a good marriage and an important factor in the choice of partner – a long established ideal. Even in arranged marriages it was expected to develop from a carefully considered compatibility, although there was a difference between parents who wanted to arrange a sensible, loving match for their child or wanted to use that child's marriage to form a useful alliance.

Canon law, by basing the validity of marriage on free consent, upheld love as a precursor of the union, and cases in the Church courts reveal that 'passionate attachment was a common experience, ... the ideal of romantic love deeply rooted in the popular culture'.[43] In 1556 a witness to a marriage contract commented that:

> it was as godlie ... as ever he was at, sayenge the same was onlie for love of both partes and without corruption.[44]

Even in the fifteenth century the language of passionate love can be found in the Paston letters and indicates the difficulty some upper-class parents may have had in getting their children to marry the intended partner.

> I pray you take good heed to my sister Anne lest the old love between her and Pampyng renew.[45]

And later in the seventeenth century the clergyman, Josselin, fell in love at first sight:

> my eye fixed with love upon a maid and hers upon me, who afterwards proved my wife.[46]

The indefinable 'it'

Such statements as that of Josselin raise the difficult question of what is this love on which so many marriages have been and are still based, related as it seems to be to the specificity of one person rather than another similarly eligible in social and economic terms. Written about since time immemorial, once the business of wizards and sorcerers and subject to aphrodisiacs, philtres and charms, and now the business of astrologers and subject to immense commercialism, it still defies exact definition. Clearly it is a well known deeply felt experience ranging on a broad spectrum from deep affection to heights and depths of passion. Thwarted love can raise the same intensity of emotion – a sense of betrayal, hatred of the betrayer and extreme jealousy of a rival. Part of the definition is that the word carries two meanings. On the one hand it denotes a caring, a compassion and delight in the other which transcends difference and carries implications of unselfishness and sacrifice. On the other hand it denotes union, loss of difference through mutual understanding and personal fulfilment through the harmony of reciprocation.

One aspect of love has been emphasised by writers as far apart as Plato:

Love is the desire and pursuit of the whole.

Coleridge:

Love is a desire of the whole being to be united to some thing or some being, felt necessary for its completeness.

Fowles, in 1977, through the words of Daniel Martin:

What I need from you is something inside you, between us, that makes half-living, half-loving ... impossible.

And, as expressed by the man in the street:

'My other half,' or even, 'My *better* half.'

In the minds of many people reciprocated love creates a sense of wholeness, the drive to love and get loved in return a search for this wholeness. In biological terms, this makes sense in that the man can experience the fullness of his masculinity and powers of reproduction only with a woman and vice versa. In psychological terms the concept also has meaning. In an attempt to make whole many people find a partner whom they perceive as complementary. The introvert may value the social skills of the extrovert who gets them both invited to and included in the party. The spontaneous may value the stability of the cautious; the cautious may value the 'life' and surprise of the spontaneous. One partner can express for a pair what the other cannot express on his own.

Other people value similarity. The extreme version of this is two people falling in love with their mirror-image – a marriage based on identification. Probably for most people the mutual attraction is a mixture of complementarity and similarity.

Some factors in mutual attraction can often be consciously

defined; certain personality characteristics, shared aspects of experience, interests, outlooks and social and economic expectations. However, we believe that unconscious motives also play a part and not only when the attraction cannot be adequately defined or rationalised and is just attributed to 'chemistry' or the indefinable 'it'.[47] These unconscious motives, which sometimes make the choice seem surprising to other people, or to the lover himself, are formed by what are often subtle aspects of previous experience of intimacy within the family of origin, often forgotten because of having happened at an early age or because of their painful nature. Most people begin their lives within an intimate relationship of bodily care and love. Within the context of the need to re-attach and the specificity of the attachment figure, referred to earlier in this chapter, the adult's capacity to love and get loved is formed in early childhood. 'We love in as much as love was present in the first great affair of our lives.'[48] People deprived of consistent and loving care in infancy seem to be incapable of love as an adult. Bowlby has stated:

> ... the kind of experience a person has, especially during childhood, greatly affects both whether he expects later to find a secure personal base, or not, and also the degree of competence he has to initiate and maintain a mutually rewarding relationship when opportunity offers. In the reverse direction the nature of the expectation a person has, and the degree of competence he brings, plays a large part in determining both the kind of person with whom he associates and how he is treated. Because of these interactions, whatever pattern is first established tends to persist.[49]

These patterns tend to persist – old lessons die hard. People whose earlier experiences of intimacy have occasioned immense pain when they have been suddenly deprived of loving care, feeling themselves to be utterly abandoned, may not dare to expose themselves to the risk of suffering that pain again. They may enter a marriage suitable in social and economic terms but one in which they and their partner unconsciously agree to avoid tangling with intense loving with its attendant risks of pain and disappointment. (It must be remembered that the greater the passion, the greater the fury and sense of betrayal when this goes wrong.)

However we take a more optimistic view than Bowlby and emphasise, as we did in Chapter 1, that unless all hope has been killed off by a series of dire environments, the psychological growth process continues to seek expression and realisation throughout life. When basic needs in respect of survival, food and shelter are assured, more refined needs seek expression. The individual, in seeking to promote the realisation of his human nature, attempts to correct earlier unsatisfactory experiences and in doing so heals old psychological wounds. We suggest that in the seemingly fateful choice of one marriage partner rather than another, just as in the choice of job, is the unconscious recognition and hope that the chosen partner can provide an environment in which there is a chance of old fears – old ghosts – being made safer, contained or even banished.

Bernard has suggested that in every marriage there are two perceived marriages: his marriage and her marriage.[50] In terms of choice of loved partner and of the expectations of the relationship, we can extend the idea to the commitment the couple make to each other. We believe there are three covenants: his covenant, her covenant and *their* unconscious covenant. The unconscious covenant includes the hope and expectation that things can be made better, but also the defence against what is most feared and the anxiety and internal conflict that this can arouse: 'Together we will try to get our internal conflict out into the external world by dividing it between us; then we will be faced with our problem and have more chance of doing something about it, but at the same time, because we are both afraid, I will protect you from knowing about your conflict, if you will protect me from knowing about mine.'

Take, for example, two young people, very attracted to each other but with a mutual problem of an inner conflict about committal of which the woman is unaware. At a conscious level she has a great investment in getting married and having a baby. She does not know about her own internal conflict as long as she can rely on the man to find all the excuses why they cannot get married now. For a time the courtship is on, then off, and then on and off again, yet they cannot get away from one another for any length of time.

If the fear is not too extreme in either of them and she can get him to overcome his conscious fear and relinquish his defence, he presumably has been reassured, but so has she. Just as she needed him to express the fear and the defence against it, so he too needed her to express the hope and the drive to overcome it. However it can happen when the fear is excessive that when he feels safer and decides he can risk 'settling down', she now finds that she has as many excuses as he had previously, and unconsciously he may pick up that he can rely on her doing this for him. As Segal has said:

> Handing feelings over to other people by actually evoking them is a kind of non-verbal communication which has great potential and is used frequently without people being aware of what they are doing. ...
> The desire to attack people, to be sarcastic or mocking or indignant or critical may be expressed by one, and the desire to protect people, to keep them safe or impotent or placated by the other. One can say 'No' all the time, and the other 'Yes' – to spending money, having sex, letting the children stay out late, lending things or whatever. One can be soft and the other hard; one mad and the other sane; one wild and the other boring. Each may use the other to express a hidden part of the self. ...
> Sometimes, as policemen using the 'hard and soft' technique, partners realise what they are doing and are grateful to the other for acting as a brake, or for giving permission for something which would be hard for themselves.[51]

Mrs Fairchild in our sample, in describing her marriage, remained puzzled by 'stupid arguments over nothing, and her occasional outbursts of 'shocking temper' into which she felt Mr Fairchild goaded her. 'He always looks for me to lose my temper,' she said.

We are speaking of the phenomenon of projection and introjection recognised and described by novelists as well as psychotherapists. In *The Genius and the Goddess*, Aldous Huxley, speaking through the voice of John Rivers, describes a sudden understanding of Kate and Henry's marriage:

> And after another paroxysm of weeping [she said], 'I haven't cried like this since before I was married.' It was only later that the full significance of that last phrase began to dawn on me. A wife who permitted herself to cry would never have done for

poor old Henry. His chronic weakness had compelled her to be unreasonably strong.[52]

We do not know why Henry could not use his strength in his marriage. (He was a genius of a scientist at work.) Nor do we know why his wife, Kate, was afraid of her own weakness and married a man who expressed this for her. However, by marrying and using each other in this way, they at least kept themselves in daily touch with that part of their unexpressed selves.

It could be said that it would be wiser to keep all the unwanted aspects of the self outside a marriage. Some people do this. All the ill, all the anger is felt to be in the big, bad world outside which then assails them – the loving pair – so cruelly. Such couples seem like 'Babes in the Wood', cuddling and keeping warm, but with their innate aggression fully repudiated and unable to muster the energy needed to deal with the normal exigencies of life.

Mr Bell, who travelled the world with a successful band, married a beautiful and much younger dancer. (They were obviously most likely to meet a prospective partner in the entertainment business.) She was attracted by the much older, seemingly competent, but 'laid back' man of the world. They were passionately in love and both of them desperately wanted a 'normal' family life which they had not known in childhood. They decided to give up their jobs as performers, start their business and have a family.

Both Mr and Mrs Bell had grown up in families in which they had been afraid of their fathers. As a child Mr Bell had been accustomed to being protected by his mother from his at times drunken, violent father. Mrs Bell's mother had not protected her from her sexually abusing one who had relegated her to the role of household drudge. She had escaped at the earliest opportunity. Consciously she married a man who she thought would look after her. However, Mr Bell, used to protection by his mother and then by the manager of the band, turned out to be an incompetent business man and, knowing little about constructive fathering, failed to provide for her and protect her in the way she wanted.

They remained very attached to each other and the 'best of friends'. At another level, Mrs Bell felt bitterly betrayed by him, but could complain about his inadequacies only behind his back. Sometimes she would throw things at him, but they both knew she would always miss her target. Sometimes she voiced her anger against her parents, but Mr Bell found this difficult to tolerate as if he could not bear to hear her speak of such sad events. Nor could he voice any anger for himself: No, he was not angry with the beautiful Mrs Bell who at times behaved in a childish and destructive way; No, he was not angry with his drunken, violent father. Yet to an observant eye, his quiet, resentful passivity, which so successfully punished Mrs Bell, belied the words.

It was not surprising that both Mr and Mrs Bell were petrified of potentially violent men. It seemed that the unconscious covenant in this marriage was to prevent Mr Bell from getting angry and, therefore, potentially violent. However, in continuing to suppress his anger, he succeeded inadvertently in suppressing his sexual desire (not an uncommon phenomenon).

In the IMS, Mr and Mrs Bell, assailed by the harsh world outside their marriage and a failed business, presented him as the one who needed treatment, but his impotence also protected Mrs Bell from her fear of sexual violence, associated as this had been in her mind with incest. When Mr Bell failed to provide economically for her he became not only the depriving father, but also the symbol of the potentially sexually abusing father. Unconsciously sex had become dangerous for them both. Ghosts were not laid to rest, but recreated and magnified through the disappointment of other facets of their relationship.

We suggest that it is wiser to keep the repudiated part of the self – or at least part of it – within the marriage. Keeping it close by affords a chance of regaining it and is a move towards becoming a fuller person. If the partner's expression of this aspect of personality is not too excessive and is seen to be used effectively, it becomes less frightening and can then be reclaimed, allowing for a more flexible balance in the marriage.

In these terms we think of the wisdom of the unconscious when it recognises and chooses to marry its own hidden problem. Or to put this in the terms we used in the last chapter, we are impressed by the ability of people to transform their environment of marriage and find in their lover a potential ally who may help them to mediate their own internal conflict on some aspect of intimacy.

Mr and Mrs Holloway felt they had a good marriage. Both of them were seemingly very independent people who, for good reasons, had doubts about the wisdom of dependency. They had shared the experience of losing their fathers by desertion in childhood, but Mr Holloway's father had reappeared when he was about to leave school and had been instrumental in finding an apprenticeship for him. This job came to symbolise his father's love for him. He was the eldest boy in the family and from an early age had taken on the role of man of the household, using his first earnings to help support the younger children. He did not feel able to marry until they were all off his hands.

Mrs Holloway bitterly resented her father's desertion because he had been her favourite parent. She saw her mother as an emotionally weak person unable to control her brothers and sisters, all of whom became delinquent. She prided herself on her strength and, despising weakness in herself and others, pulled herself up by her boot straps, got herself a further education and a good job. She was rigidly self-sufficient.

She came to love Mr Holloway because, as she said, he was unlike her father; he was strong, a 'brick wall', safe and reliable. Within this safety she was able to risk some dependency on him and slowly became less rigid in her self-sufficiency. However their marriage continued to depend on the joint assumption that he always had to be the strong one. She had got herself a bit more whole. He had not, but he obtained gratification from her softening and from his ability to do for her what his father had failed to do for him.

Mr Treacher also found salvation in his wife as well as in his job as an apron manager. When his father had 'rubbished' him as a child, his mother had said, 'Come with me. I'm going to do the shopping.' He became very dependent on her. He wisely married a woman on whom he could continue to depend on being there when he wanted her to be – a safe attachment figure; Mrs Treacher suffered a mild agoraphobia which kept her much of the time home-based. However she behaved in a different way from his mother in that she said, 'We can do it,' and 'You can do it.' Mr Treacher did not feel rubbished and under her tutelage claimed his own strength and became a competent person. We do not know Mrs Treacher's early history, but agoraphobia suggests that she had strong attachment needs which had not previously been fulfilled. Fortunately she did not need to project her weakness into Mr Treacher. In their intense attachment they were a couple whose 'double bed sagged well in the middle'.

However some marriages can become very distressed when the mutual projective system gets 'over-played', because the strength of the fear turns out to be stronger than the hope that the internal conflict can be ameliorated. When the recipient of the projection carries his own impulse and that of the projector as well over an extended period, we say he is carrying a 'double dose' of feeling. The overt expression of this in the behaviour becomes more pronounced and, therefore, even more frightening to the one who is ridding himself of that feeling. When this happens, what first attracted one person to another can become the main cause of complaint.

Mr and Mrs Becker were both lonely people and unsure of their own identity and personal worth. Mr Becker had experienced his parents as insisting on his achieving just for their benefit. Mrs Becker was confused; she felt she got her mother's attention only by working hard and doing well, but her father had constantly advised her not to get above herself.

Consciously they had been drawn together by their differences. It was as if they could define themselves only in opposition to another. Mrs Becker, unconsciously attempting to please both parents, was serious and conscientious, although never allowing herself to succeed beyond a certain point. Only in this way did she think she might get herself valued. She, who had never dared to rebel, was attracted by the anti-work, anti-success Mr Becker who by this time had rejected his parents' aspirations and was mixing with 'drop-outs'. He was attracted by her conformity and reliability.

Despite a continual disappointment in each other, they stayed in their marriage, a satisfying sexual relationship uniting the rebel and the conformer. When, in their early thirties, the issue of whether they should have a baby or not came to the fore, their fears of being taken over by each other (and by a baby) increased, as did their accompanying projective defences. His way of life became less tolerable to her and the more she complained, the more rebellious he became. The more he rebelled, the more sensible she felt she had to be. With his carrying all the rebellion for them both, and her carrying all the good sense, nothing they said or did in their difference could please the other. On the odd occasion when she agreed with him, he immediately changed his stance.

Mr and Mrs Becker used their differences to confirm their own weak sense of identity, to ensure a distance between them and to avoid any prolonged intimacy which they felt to be too threatening to their sense of self. The issue in any marriage is how much intimacy without throttling the other, how much togetherness and how much separateness.

For the last 200 years or so, employment outside the home has provided for most people a convenient way of being separate for much of the day. In the previous chapter we looked at the latent functions of work for the individual, first at a general level – the five functions listed by Jahoda – and second, the idiosyncratic, personal level by which people transform the experience of work through sublimation and a variety of symbols to serve their own psychological needs. In the final part of this chapter we extend the idea of latent functions of work and see how this can be applied not just to the individual, but to a marriage and a marriage partner.

'The morning that separates'*

In all modern marriages there is a tension between the needs of the partnership and the needs of the individual. On the one hand, by marrying, people seek intimacy and togetherness; on the other hand, they need separateness and room for experiencing aspects of their personality not always possible in the company of their partner. The concept of psychological distance and the problems of intimacy have been graphically described by Schopenhauer's story of the porcupines, later quoted by Freud:[53]

> A company of porcupines crowded themselves together one cold winter's day so as to profit by one another's warmth and so save themselves from being frozen to death. But soon they felt one another's quills, which induced them to separate again. And

* T.S. Eliot, *The Cocktail Party*.

now, when the need for warmth brought them nearer together again, the second evil arose once more, so that they were driven backwards and forwards from one trouble to the other, until they discovered a mean distance at which they could most tolerably exist.

In modern Britain, although often governed by tradition, people can, if they choose, exercise considerable discretion as to how they conduct their private lives and the amount of physical togetherness and separateness they wish to maintain. The balance that is appropriate for one couple may be different from that of another and any newly married couple may need, like the porcupines, to work out by trial and error what is appropriate for them. As Rilke has said, 'A good marriage is that which appoints the other guardian of his solitude.' And in the words of Khalil Gibran: '... let there be spaces in your togetherness. And let the winds of heaven dance between you.'

Byng Hall,[54] in writing about distance in marriage, says:

> Many marriages may seem too close and suffocating at times; at other times they may feel too distant and remote. Spouses need to know and heed these signs.

In the same context, he describes an adequate marriage:

> ... there will be periods of intimacy, safe in the knowledge that it will not become too intrusive. Interspersed with these will be periods of greater autonomy that are also protected by the knowledge that the relationship will not be allowed to become too tenuous and that the other person will be available when closeness is needed – a safe base to which to return.

Employment, mainly outside the home as we have known it since the industrial revolution, is one of the main areas of life which enables a married couple to achieve structured distance from each other – physical distance, social distance through different sets of relationships and, when the job provides stimulus, intellectual difference.* De Riencourt,[55] writing

---

* It is an interesting question whether we have just become conditioned to this amount of separation; whether in periods of history when marriage roles were more integrated, spouses managed one way or another to find their own space; or whether in the present emphasis on fulfilment of the self, separateness has become a more important issue than previously.

about the position of women in history and the family no longer being a productive economic unit, says,

> But something far more dangerous was taking place stealthily: the sexes were moving at full speed away from one another in all realms, except that of physical relations, because the ever expanding *machine* had interposed itself between them.

Speaking of the technological husband and a non-technological wife with little to say to each other, he continued:

> The full scale flight into specialisation and the increasingly abstruse nature of these special fields of interest have raised the conjugal barriers higher still; in an age of growing specialisation, increasing gender specialisation became inevitable.

He asked:

> What kind of society advises young, ambitious executives that 'the man who goes to the top has got to be slightly dissatisfied with his marriage' and 'should be able to put his marriage in "neutral" when his job becomes unusually demanding'? Or that 'the really successful business executive has distressingly little time for his family' and that 'if you want a full home life, you'd better be content with a lesser job?'

Some jobs are known as 'greedy' occupations, and in many occupations, whether greedy or not, most main breadwinners for the family will at times experience considerable conflict between demands of work and demands and needs of the family. However, occupations not necessarily greedy can be made so, particularly by men who find their principal source of identity in their work rather than in their marriage and family life; ambition and, therefore, career can be put first with a willingness to work as many and more hours than the job demands, expecting wife and family to fit around this and wives to manage every aspect of life at home.[56] Employment, sometimes creating marital problems, may also be used as a haven from them or from marital boredom. Work has been called the 'acceptable mistress', often suffered by wives and regularly complained about, but not with the same anguish that an actual lover would evoke.

Some jobs require the employee to be absent from home intermittently either for short or long periods. The question needs to be asked, why, when choice is available, do people choose occupations which take them away for extended periods. Clark *et al*., in studying the 'problematic consequences of intermittent husband absence' for marriages in which the husband worked in the off-shore oil industry, found that despite the current high unemployment rate, 'a fairly large degree of self-selection seems to be operational, since over one third (37%) of the men had previous jobs which also involved working away from home'.[57]

Those who had changed from on-shore to off-shore jobs often saw this as a temporary expedient, the higher level of income acquired sought purposefully to finance a family project such as buying a larger or better house. However some couples stressed that work away from home actually gave them more time together: 'Although I'm away a fortnight, I'm going to see an awful lot more of my family in my fortnight at home.' His wife endorsed this view: 'You can make better use of your time together.'

One wife, valuing the arrangement, remarked: 'We get on much better together with his absence ... you can really tell that he does appreciate you more than if you were living day to day, each month, each year.'

We had only two couples in our samples in which the husband's job took him regularly away for extended periods. Mrs Roker enjoyed the 'comings and goings' of her soldier husband from their married quarters. Mr and Mrs Underwood were clearly and consciously using his occupation of sailor to limit their involvement. Mrs Underwood was first attracted to Mr Underwood on account of the exciting and philandering life she imagined he led as he voyaged round the world. Mr Underwood was obviously a restless person, unable to handle close relationships and settle in one place. However, he longed for an 'ideal' home and a secure base to which to return from time to time. His job served them both well. He could keep his home 'ideal', his 'pride and joy', as long as he was not there too often, nor long enough to put the ideal to the test. Like Mr Treacher (whose wife was agoraphobic) he knew the unadventurous Mrs Underwood would be there when he needed her. She, having always lived a circumscribed life and

unable to create her own excitement, kept this 'dangerous' part
of herself on the horizon with her continued fantasies about his
exciting, sexual ventures, of which she was apparently not the
least jealous. (Perhaps she knew they were a product of her
imagination.)

In a less structured way, Mr Kettlewell used his occupation
to absent himself from his wife and family whenever the
situation at home looked as if it would require more of his time
and attention. He worked exceptionally long hours as a prison
warder, but when his wife or a child was ill, he always
managed to *have* to take on extra duties; he was the first to
offer himself. When Mrs Kettlewell had a minor nervous
breakdown, he applied for a transfer to another prison at the
far end of the country, leaving her alone with three small
children. He portrayed himself as a 'tough guy' but, when the
'going got tough' at home, he was away.

However, many of our couples, unlike those described by
Gorer quoted earlier in this chapter, achieved considerable
separation by exercising clear traditional, complementary
roles in their marriages, particularly in the Tyneside area.
Much of this was culturally determined; they conducted their
lives as their parents had done. Husbands were full-time
earners, gardeners and allotment diggers and found their
social life with other men in pub or club. Wives were the
homemakers and full-time mothers, only taking jobs when the
children were at school. Men's work and life was outside the
home, women's inside it. Territory was clearly defined and
sharing of task or role was not a predominant characteristic of
these marriages.

One middle-class couple, Mr and Mrs Parker, carried role
differentiation to extremes, but this seemed to have less to do
with tradition than with an unconscious covenant that one
person could succeed only at the expense of another and Mr
Parker's fear that if he were not careful 'women' would take
over. (In his family of origin, his mother had made all the
decisions.) It was not clear whether he was in a 'greedy'
occupation, or used it as such, but Mrs Parker certainly saw it
as being so and resented his being late in the evening or away
for the odd night. Not only was he the sole earner, but also the
sole decision maker. Although Mrs Parker prided herself on
being a good mother, housekeeper and manager, for many

years she was not 'allowed' a cheque book, nor to exercise any independence.

She rarely complained, but stored up years of resentment that he 'used' her and had pursued his career at her expense. Mr Parker had been the only member of his family to acquire a higher education. Mrs Parker had been the one member of her family not to get to grammar school. She continued to direct her resentment about this on to her husband and experienced any talk of his colleagues' working wives as a 'putting down'. Mr Parker remained oblivious that his wife was so dissatisfied.

The Rokers, Underwoods, Kettlewells and Parkers were exceptions in our sample in that the husband's occupation was blatantly used as a means of distancing either with accompanying delight and satisfaction, or resentment, or, as in the case of Mrs Kettlewell, with resignation. The majority of couples in our two samples had been conditioned to and used the husband's structured employment outside the home as a means of daily separation without undue psychological abuse or motive. How necessary it had become to them, however, only became apparent when the husband became redundant and they were deprived of the usual means of obtaining some distance from each other for part of the day. In Chapter 7 we describe the difficulties that many of them experienced when they had too much togetherness day-in, day-out.

The days that held together

In contrast to the many couples who used employment to get apart for much of the day, a few couples in our samples were in the same profession and worked together. Mr and Mrs Norton, both linguists, used their shared work experience as the 'glue that held them together'. Their marriage was seemingly built on a work contract. Mrs Norton was explicit about how frightened she felt when left on her own on the few occasions when work took Mr Norton out of her presence for a day. However, meal times were problematic for them; she always wanted to continue to work and talk about the day's plans and activities. He, expressing for both of them some, if not much, need for separation, preferred to read classics, Greek at breakfast, Latin at lunch and Chinese at dinner.

Mr and Mrs Nugent were another couple who were both in

the same occupation, her position slightly senior to his. She was attracted by his casual attitude to life, the opposite of her serious intent, but they were firmly united not only by their shared occupational interest but also by a number of joint 'againsts'; together they were against this system, that system, this religion and that political view. Like Mr and Mrs Bell, described earlier in this chapter, all their anger was projected out of the marriage into the bad world outside. They both worked on renovating their house and she enjoyed the scrimping and saving they needed to do on their fairly low salaries. They pulled together in the purpose she so strongly expressed for them both.

Starting a family and Mrs Nugent becoming a full-time mother was part of the long-term plan. In anticipation of her ceasing to earn, he would seek the promotion he had previously despised. The plan came to fruition; two children were born and Mr Nugent moved quickly up the occupational ladder. Financially they were now secure. Yet Mrs Nugent, unable to redefine her role as wife and mother with any satisfaction and considering herself as unemployed, could not bear the physical and intellectual separation. He was often late home, tired and with little energy for her and the children. He was bemused by her complaint as he was doing exactly what they had planned. Eventually she left him, but then put herself in a situation of struggle, similar to the earlier days of her marriage to him.

Two wives in our sample were instrumental in their husbands' unemployment, a crisis in the marriage relationship inappropriately handled by the wife in her insistence that the husband give up his job. Mr and Mrs Stradwick had had their marital problems over the years, but spoke of a period when he had been in regular employment as one of stability in their marriage. At the point in time we learnt of them, the two children would soon be leaving home. Mrs Stradwick complained of boredom, and then she and Mr Stradwick precipitated an exciting crisis. Mr Stradwick boasted that his boss's wife had kissed him. Mrs Stradwick insisted that he left his job and 'because of the shame', gave up her own job as barmaid in the village pub. After a subsequent row, he burgled the pub. Mrs Stradwick had her excitement, but then seemed much happier when she decided he was to be self-employed at home. The so-called self-employment had little reality and Mr

Stradwick resentfully complained to his probation officer that Mrs Stradwick would not let him work; his previous boss would have him back, he said.

Vicarious occupational identity

Mrs Stradwick did not apparently rely on her husband's job to define her status. This is unusual. In Chapter 2 we referred to occupation as a main definer of social status for both man and wife. Earlier in this chapter we noted that working-class women are economically and socially dependent on marriage as a 'career', a husband's earnings likely to be so much higher than his wife's. Despite the bigger choice and possibilities open to them, even middle-class women tend to be married to their husbands' careers in terms of the priority given to them over their own. It is a very small percentage of women who move through their own careers to the top jobs. (In Britain only 8.3% of general management jobs are held by women.[58] A recent report indicated that 'work bias' costs women fifteen billion pounds a year. They do not have access to overtime or bonus rates or unsocial hours payment. In respect of manual work, men, in total, receive two and a half times the income received by women. In non-manual work, 42,000 women earn more than £15,600 compared with one million men.[59]) Once they give up a job to start and care for a family they lose ground in a competitive market and in many trades they have to prove themselves to be more competent than their male counterparts to achieve the same level of promotion.[60]

Some occupations are exceptionally greedy in that there is an expectation that the wife will not just support the husband, but will be actively involved in his work without remuneration. A wife in the Diplomatic Service 'can spend so much time on embassy work that she may feel like an unpaid employee'.[61] One wife, commenting on her life as a diplomat's wife, said, 'Rank is very prevalent, so you become the Second Secretary's wife, for example, and there is a big divide between junior and senior wives.'[62] It is not unknown for army wives to speak of *our* regiment', as clergymen's wives sometimes refer to *our* parish'.[63]

Some modern wives of men in this type of occupation complain about the expectation of their unpaid helpmate-role and, for example, that people relate to them only as 'the vicar's wife'. Others find satisfaction in putting their energies into their husband's work. As Finch,[64] in her study of clergymen's wives, states:

> There are real benefits as well as losses to be derived from incorporation into one's husband's work. ... since wives are denied full (and often partial) participation in many sources of potential satisfaction available to men, the opportunity to engage in the public domain via their husband's work may serve to expand their otherwise very limited opportunities.

There has been some shift in attitude over the past twenty years in that some businesses and professions now find that they are losing good men, or that men are foregoing promotion, when this involves yet once again a move to another part of the country. This opting out seems to be related to the wives' protests and a weighing up of the interests of all members of the family – the possibility of the wife's finding employment in her own line and the children's schooling. It also accompanies the massive change from rented to owner occupation.

However, as long as the majority of married women 'take a job' as opposed to pursuing their own careers, their employment accommodating their husbands' employment and domestic concerns, it is not surprising that a husband's type of employment defines a wife's social status. His employment and promotions provide a more consistent strand through the years than her own.

In our two samples just over half (29) of the marriages were traditional; the wives were home-based, domestic work and child care supporting the husband's employment before redundancy (or in one or two cases, self-inflicted unemployment) took place. Of the 28 working wives, 20 (out of 25) were in the clinical, mainly middle-class sample, only 9 (out of 34) in the workshop sample which had a much wider spread of social class. No wives were incorporated in their husband's employment. Professional women were under-represented (14), and with no couple did the wife's career take precedence over that of her husband. 21 wives had returned to paid employment outside the home after the birth of children, 11 full-time, 10 part-time.

Some of these women in full or part-time employment before or after the birth of children found intrinsic satisfaction in their jobs but were not actively pursuing their way to the top. Some wives were explicit that they needed to work not just for financial reasons. Mrs Pierce, for example, was depressed after the birth of her child and on her doctor's advice took a job but, as statistically prevalent, in a less responsible position than she had previously held.

We learnt less about the personal meaning of work for the wives, as in the consultancy or helping situation the emphasis was on the husband's loss of job. The wives, in relating to this loss, perceived their husbands as victims and, not wanting to increase their distress, spoke less about their own jobs. In addition, although they were concerned about doing their jobs well and obtaining satisfaction from them, it was their husband's employment which they used as a social definer, as it is officially recorded by the Registrar General.

Sexual differentiation

In the last chapter we described how jobs which overtly defined masculinity were clearly important for some husbands in our sample. We described Mr Skelton's fear of puniness and emphasis on heavy work, and Mr Todd's use of his job to escape from his mother's clutches and to establish himself as a man in his own right. Another husband, Mr Walton, was promoted from an outside job he did well to an inside one behind a desk. Despite his pride in his promotion, he felt less of a man – 'just inadequate', he said.

Earlier in this chapter we noted how identity defined by role and territory – men's work and leisure outside the home, women's work inside the home – enabled some couples to achieve distance and separation from each other, much of this apparently culturally determined. It also served to emphasise sexual differentiation. For those men who had a fragile sense of sexual identity, confirmation of gender in the work role also provided confirmation within the marriage and was important for many wives. In the unconscious choice of partner, fragility of sexual identity married similar fragility.

Mr Todd needed Mrs Todd's drive and courtship to wean him away from his mother. In both their families mothers were dominant. Mrs Todd was the second eldest of a very large family with an alcoholic father. She had to help her mother bring up the younger children and in her experience it was women who bore all the responsibility while men were competent only at impregnation. Mr Todd's steady job helped him to claim his manhood, but also allowed her to be less managing.

Mrs Holloway despised her 'weak' mother and was more identified with her father who had deserted. Married to the strong, safe, 'brick-wall' Mr Holloway, she could slowly allow herself some dependency and show the softer side of her personality.

Mrs Pierce had been bullied by her father until one day she realised she was bigger than he. This discovery changed her life and she became another assertive woman, intent on not showing her vulnerability. Mr Pierce had wanted to be a hairdresser, but his family insisted he did something more 'manly'. He eventually ended up in a senior management position. This was important to Mrs Pierce who had severe doubts about her own femininity. As long as he was symbolically the more powerful (who did not hit her), she could experience some of her femininity, although as we mentioned earlier in this chapter, she was not comfortable in the role of mother of a young baby. However, her discomfort increased when he, made redundant and not short of money, settled in at home and took on the role of house-person which she had found difficulty in sustaining. Rows always started with her agitating that he 'did' something.

Use of their toughness at work enabled some men in our sample to exercise the softer, caring aspects of their personality at home. Mr Morrison, for example, was seen by the health visitor as the 'ideal' father who took a handsome share of the care of the child when he was home. However, his behaviour was no longer seen as ideal by his wife and the health visitor when he was unemployed.

Sublimation outside the marriage

In the last chapter we added a sixth function with a different dimension to Jahoda's list of latent functions of work: sublimation — the absorption of aggressive and other potentially destructive impulses. This was important for many marriages in that containment and modification at work kept these impulses out of the marriage. This explanation can also be related to Mr Morrison's changed behaviour when he no longer had a formalised outlet for his aggression.

Mr Murray was in a high-powered and thrusting role in the oil business which provided him with a channel through which he could make constructive use of his highly aggressive and competitive qualities.

He and his wife thought their marriage was good when he was in work and neither felt in competition with the other. Mr and Mrs Norton, the two linguists, were highly competitive with each other, but while they were both employed, their competitiveness was restricted to this area of their life and promoted their professional competence. When they were both unemployed, it became a destructive source of marital tension.

Mr Kettlewell's job in the prison service, containing potentially violent prisoners, was important for his marriage and, as long as he was working in this type of job, he and Mrs Kettlewell were able to have sex. Again, it was a different story when he was unemployed, as it was with the Morrisons, the Murrays and the Nortons.

The couples we have described came into our sample only when one or both partners were unemployed (or the unemployment was pending) and they sought help or came to the attention of a practitioner. Thus what they told us about their marriage in relation to past employment was mainly retrospective. We did not find that they unduly idealised either their marriage or the job. However, it was when a job was lost that the latent functions of employment in respect of a marriage – provision of structured distance, confirmation of gender identity and an external channel for sublimation and symbolisation – were exposed. In the next part of the book we address this subject of loss.

Part II

LOSS OF JOB

There is always talk of politics and campaigning, but nobody really wants to talk about individual problems, be they financial or emotional. Sometimes it feels as if the politicians are talked of to avoid knowing about individuals.

An unemployed husband

4

Signals

I have only one eye – I have the right to be blind sometimes: ... I really do not see the signal!

Nelson

In this part of the book about loss of job and its effects on marriages, we describe some common themes and changed patterns of marital interaction between husbands and wives that emerged from our clinical and workshop samples.

Seeking help one way or another

Couples in our samples, by definition of their being clients, had a problem. They had either approached or accepted a referral to a practitioner, or they or one of their children had done something which brought them into contact with one. However this does not mean that at the first contact they expressed their trouble in terms of being unemployed *and* of having a marital problem, nor of just one or the other.

Mr and Mrs Roker, for example, asked for no help and thought the school was making an unnecessary fuss when the head teacher asked to see them and expressed concern to them and to the health visitor about their seven-year-old child's stealing from under the teacher's eyes. They thought the school should exert more discipline. However the child's stealing ceased when the health visitor took note of Mr Roker's unemployment and invited the couple to talk about it. Only then did she learn of the changes in their relationship which left Mrs Roker so uncomfortable. In this case, the child had sent out the signal.

Mr and Mrs Treacher, described in Chapters 2 and 3, asked for help through Mr Treacher's suicide attempt. At first he could not say what was wrong, other than 'everything was useless'. Only when his wife had spoken of her anxiety about soon going into hospital, could he also speak of this and of his changed work circumstances. Through thirty years of marriage Mrs Treacher had been his support, guide, mentor and encourager. They had enjoyed much physical contact and, as the reader may remember, their double bed 'sagged well in the middle'. Recently they had become isolated from each other; physically isolated, sleeping in separate bedrooms for fear of his hurting her; and emotionally isolated, unable to hear each other's distress about illness, feared death and, therefore, final separation – a marital problem which accentuated Mr Treacher's disturbing feelings about losing his authority at work and then taking an offered redundancy. He felt 'useless' – literally redundant – but also petrified.

Mr and Mrs Treacher's social worker, specialising in psychiatric work in a general hospital, explained to the workshop:

> I get stuck in the illness model. A man becomes ill because that is actually better than being unemployed.
>
> And I've found that when it's the wife who is depressed the husband sees it as a way of establishing a role for himself. So I am tussling with, 'Your wife is not ill.' But he says, 'Oh, it's OK to stay in bed till 10 and I'll bring you a cup of tea.' And during this time he has nipped round with the vacuum cleaner and decided what they are going to have for lunch and then says, 'Why don't you have a bath. You don't have to get dressed straight away.' And all of a sudden we've got this really sick woman.

Mr Streatfield explicitly asked for help for himself in court. He got into trouble, he said, because of his drinking which, he realised, changed his behaviour. He was spending all the money and causing the stress in his family. He made no connection between his changed behaviour and his being unemployed. In Tyneside, unemployment was a fact of life. To the probation officer he described himself as 'stupid' and inadequate and needing the support of his wife. She confirmed this view. She complained that during the week he sat all day in his chair watching the TV and he did not help her in the house. 'But, when I do,' he said, 'she complains that I'm not doing it properly.' Not unexpectedly, the 'You're not doing it properly' Mrs Streatfield was ultra efficient and made a habit of finishing off Mr Streatfield's slow sentences. When the probation officer suggested something he might do, she was quick to respond that he would not be capable. The probation officer enlisted her as another helper and suggested a plan for a family outing over the weekend. It failed to happen. Mr Streatfield spent the money on alcohol once more. 'I told you so,' were the triumphant words of Mrs Streatfield.

As a condition of his probation order, Mr Streatfield started to attend a day centre. His punctuality, his pleasure in getting out each morning, his ability to learn a new skill and his facilitating and teaching capacity with younger men at the centre indicated that the 'stupid' Mr Streatfield was by no means workshy nor so stupid. Mrs Streatfield had complained of his 'rubbish' – his keeping her awake at nights when he talked of his loneliness and of being out of work, and of his being accepted by his drinking mates and now by the men at the day centre. With the probation officer's help his 'rubbish' got upgraded to serious conversation about both their feelings. But the question remained unanswered why Mrs Streatfield had to be quite so castrating and so efficient at his expense and, as it later turned out, tacitly encouraging his weekend drinking, giving herself the opportunity to spend that time with her own parents.

The probation officer could have said, 'I am stuck in the offence model'. Mr and Mrs Streatfield did not complain about his unemployment nor their marital problem. Yet Mr Streatfield's behaviour at the day centre suggested that his drinking problem and the offence he committed while under its influence was related to his unemployment. They displayed their marital problem in the interviews with the probation officer each time Mrs Streatfield cut Mr Streatfield down to size.

This indirect way of displaying a marital problem to a practitioner is not exceptional. Rather, it is unusual in services not specialising in marital work for clients to ask for help with their troubled marriage for its own sake. A study of 1,198 cases referred to a social services department in one year showed that

Battered wives required accommodation and deserted husbands day care facilities on the grounds of their marital difficulties, but this was a far cry from requesting the social worker to intervene in their marital affairs. Two or three cases within the 1,198 could be seen as requests to the social worker to carry out marital work as a means of reducing other problems (depression or alcoholism) and other cases left the social workers scope for deciding whether or not they would consider working with the marital problem. In these latter cases it seemed that the social workers often chose to concentrate on the immediate practical difficulties.[1]

At the Intake stage in this study the number of cases having an overt marital problem was small. 'In only 3% did the social worker think it worth mentioning.' Yet marital problems were much more common in caseloads and said to be almost universal among the married clients to whom the social workers were giving priority.

Similarly, health visitors are often not told in the first instance of a marital problem and in 'the baby care model' the signal is first given through the children. In terms of the agency's assigned task, this can be seen as appropriate signalling.

When Mr Morrison had been employed, the health visitor had perceived him and his wife as an 'ideal' couple, requiring only statutory, routine visits. A year after Mr Morrison became unemployed, Mrs Morrison sent up an increasing number of signals that all was not well. The care of the children was clearly deteriorating. Mrs Morrison explained carefully that she was deliberately giving them a stodgy diet in order to keep them drowsy. Then the previously 'good' husband and father was described as not so good. And then, wanting to make the message even clearer, Mr and Mrs Morrison started to bicker, then quarrel and then fight in front of her.

The majority of marital problems are in the first instance taken to GPs,[2] who like Mr and Mrs Treacher's social worker are stuck in the illness model. Pugh and Cohen studied fourteen cases in which in retrospect the consultation with the GP was found to be primarily about marital difficulties.[3] Yet they found that not one of these patients initially presented this problem as the reason for the consultation. Higgs, writing of *Life Changes*[4] said (somewhat ruefully), 'We do not know what really brings a patient to a doctor.' And Beale and Nethercote, writing on *Job Loss and Family Morbidity*[5] and commenting on the reluctance of the unemployed to admit to their predicament, stated:

> Many consultations are unsatisfactory because the real reason for the consultation does not emerge and there is an increased risk of chronicity. The results of this study lend credence to this for redundancy was only recorded in a minority of cases.

Mr and Mrs Yardley were not in our sample, but Mr Yardley had recently retired and, therefore, they were in a comparable position. Mrs Yardley tried to tell her husband that all was not well. When she failed to get him to listen and he failed to hear, she signalled their GP for help through symptoms of hypertension. The specialist to whom she was referred helped her and her husband re-define the problem in relationship terms and then re-referred them to the IMS. Mr Yardley, although still doubtful whether his wife's symptoms were related to their marital problem, could describe on an application form the connection between their joint problem and his having ceased work. He wrote:

> The problem seems to be one of communication; not a breakdown in communication, because we have always tended to be rather silent – but an awareness that the absence of talk is likely to affect us both now that I have retired.
>
> While I was working we had breakfast and washed up to the accompaniment of Radio 3 music, listening for the time checks to indicate when I should leave for the train, and little needed to be said. Having returned home in the evening, we ate our meal to the accompaniment of the 6 pm news and again little needed to be said or was said apart from the exchange of snippets of information from the domestic or office scenes. Now that I no longer go to the office one source of such talk has dried up.
>
> Provided I have known that the domestic silence was nothing to do with my being 'in the dog house' it has not bothered me much in the past, because during the working week we lived our separate lives and I accepted that we were neither of us real talkers. But even I can see that prolonged silence in retirement could become a problem.
>
> As you can perhaps see, I prefer the written word to the spoken one.

Not surprisingly, couples attending sexual dysfunction clinics were explicit about their sexual problems, but did not relate them to the husband's unemployment. Mr Kettlewell maintained that there was nothing really wrong other than that he could not perform. He and Mrs Kettlewell were happy, had no other problems and all the children were grown up and away from home, but remained devoted to them. He thought his non-performance was all his fault and he wondered why the doctor and social worker, co-therapists, wanted to see Mrs Kettlewell as well as him. He thought he must be lacking in vitamins or hormones and all that he needed was a quick injection.

In an interview on her own, Mrs Kettlewell confessed to years of unhappiness before Mr Kettlewell was discharged from the prison service. Then he had visibly lost confidence and had become impotent within a fortnight; 'then he wouldn't even try'. And he had become more withdrawn than previously, but she was reluctant to share her unhappiness with her husband. She did not want to bring up what had happened in the past. He was unemployed now, she said: 'Please don't rock the boat.'

The two therapists did not make much headway with the underlying marital problem. However Mr Kettlewell regained his erection after he had obtained another job as a bailiff. Mrs Kettlewell wanted to continue with the counselling, but he was less sure.

The practitioner who worked with Mr and Mrs Kettlewell told the workshop,

> I was quite surprised when I looked through my current caseload to find from the top of my head *ten couples with one partner unemployed*. The interesting thing is that they come to us, not because they are unemployed, but because they've got a sexual problem which they don't see as being related to the unemployment until we look at it. People come to the doctor because they've got a specific complaint; that is OK.

Couples who went of their own accord or were referred to a marriage guidance council more usually expressed their problem in marital terms, but not always in the first instance. Mr and Mrs Rowlands spoke first of the trouble their

19-year-old son was causing them. The tension in the room was at its highest when they spoke of him. Either one or other of them had taken it upon themselves to boot him out at various times, but Mrs Rowlands had always encouraged or manoeuvred him back, yet continued to feel a 'pig in the middle' between him and her husband. Encouraged to talk more about themselves and less about the boy, it became clear that, although their problem was of long standing, a row about their son and other frustrations had precipitated Mrs Rowlands into making the appointment for them. That Mr Rowlands had been unemployed for six years was not seen by them as a relevant factor, although they associated that as a cause of a depression he had had, leaving him with an 'inability to cope with normal life crises'. They had not connected any of their troubles to their abnormally high expectations of each other, of their children, and of jobs and the status of those jobs which had led Mr Rowlands to leave his work in the first place and contributed to his failure to find another job.

Mr and Mrs Fairchild were referred to the IMS, came to the initial consultation and then proclaimed they had *no* problem. The shock of the loss of Mr Fairchild's job and the circumstances preceding this had drawn them closer together. They were managing remarkably well, making a purposeful adjustment to each other in their reduced circumstances. They were communicating in a way they had not done previously and were experiencing more intimacy together than they had ever known before. We wondered why they had accepted the referral and then our offer of a treatment vacancy, and what it was they had not been able to tell us other than their concern about the practical problems they now faced together. Near the end of the regular sessions, Mrs Fairchild likened the process to 'going to the dentist – not aware of a problem, learning of a cavity, finding the treatment painful and then feeling better'. Why did they stick with the painful process if they had no problem? They arrived punctually for each session. It was as if two sets of feet, led by their unconscious or some vague disquiet, rather than their intellectual appreciation of their relationship, had brought them to the agency.

In contrast, Mr and Mrs Bell, also referred to the IMS, were explicit about the connection between their marital problem

When it comes to sex I freeze ... .

and their unemployment:

> The problem as I see it is that we see each other too much from
> the time we met four years ago up to now. We have seen each
> other 24 hours a day.

And finally in this sample of signals, Mr Little drew attention
to himself and his marital problem loud and clear. An initial
pastoral visit (one of many in a notorious street used as a
dumping ground by the housing authority for problem families,
graffiti abounding, giro cheques stolen from the postman,
floorboards used for firewood, and where a clean doorstep or
window was derided) elicited that when a child Mr Little had
been a choirboy. He was invited to join again. On his first
attendance at church at the 'tea and get together' after the
service he was, on the instigation of the vicar, befriended by a
member of the congregation. She introduced herself. 'Hullo. My
name is Sheila. What is yours?' 'My name is Tom,' he replied in
a loud voice, 'and I cannot stand my wife. I cannot bear her.' He
did not add, 'And I am unemployed.' The vicar duly picked up
this blatant signal and made another home visit.

The struggle of the past

We are not arguing that loss of work turns otherwise satisfying
marriages bad. Mr and Mrs Fairchild, in fact, had a marital
problem before his loss of work. The shock of this and their
basic need of each other brought them closer together. They,
however, were an exception. For most of our couples, the shock
of the loss of work and continued unemployment exposed
immaturities or problems in their way of relating which
previously with the help of work, an adequate or near adequate
income, a structured day and the means of distancing the
husband and wife for probably eight hours or so for five days a
week had been contained.

Mr and Mrs Rowlands were pleased with each other before
Mr Rowlands' unemployment, and Mrs Rowlands particularly
valued his humour. But Mr Rowlands' problem of seeking jobs
with more status than his apparent ability allowed was

presumably a factor in his personality and could have affected them even if he had remained in work but continued to be dissatisfied with himself. We do not know whether, if he had continued in employment, he and his wife would have found it easier to let their son grow up and leave home.

Mr Treacher's job of apron manager (parking aeroplanes) altered its character about the same time as his wife's health deteriorated. Both his marriage and his job had supported his immature personality so that he functioned well, although obsessively. He was threatened with the loss of two major props in his life. Feeling that 'everything was useless', he took an overdose. And then, Mrs Treacher's physical symptoms became ominous – 'nasties inside her'. She was admitted to hospital. By this time Mr Treacher had taken an offered redundancy and, in the social worker's words, was 'the first man to be admitted to a psychiatric unit from a gynaecological ward'. When visiting Mrs Treacher, he had one of what later came to be called his 'wobblies'. In his distress (Mrs Treacher did not seem to be properly 'parked' in the ward as she was at home), he kicked the bed, stamped his feet, tore at his hair, shouted and screamed and generally caused mayhem in an otherwise peaceable ward.

Mr and Mrs Streatfield had a massive marital problem when the probation officer first met them. When he could escape from his castrating wife into the day centre, Mr Streatfield proved himself able. Before that facility was available to him, he escaped to the support of his drinking mates. His drinking problem appeared to be more related to the need to get out and for male company than to the actual alcohol. He went back on a drinking bout the weekend after he had served his time in the day centre. We do not know, however, whether, when he was a provider, Mrs Streatfield had had to be quite so castrating nor when he was out of the house on five working days a week, whether she had had to retreat quite so regularly to the safety of her parents' home.

Mr and Mrs Morrison's marital problem arose when he had been unemployed for over a year. We cannot say it was caused only by the unemployment despite the fact that they were described as an 'ideal' couple when he was employed. No doubt, the way he and his wife dealt with their changed circumstances was consistent with their basic personality characteristics in dealing with loss, change and stress. Mr Morrison had served an apprenticeship. He had enjoyed his actual work and the masculine environment of the dockyard. He had earned good money. They had lost financial resources and an image of him as a competent worker and provider.

One of their problems when he was made redundant was that they could not let themselves know about the implications of the redundancy or the feelings of loss which would be considered normal in the circumstances. When he was employed they had bought their own house and started a family. Their one child, Pamela, was three years old and they were hoping to conceive another baby when Mr Morrison became redundant. Confident that he would soon find another job, they decided to go ahead with this decision and before long Mrs Morrison was pregnant. Mr Morrison did not find another job, despite his skill and despite his numerous attempts, but he remained hopeful and buoyant even though he was as unsuccessful as were most of his previous workmates in an area of high unemployment.

In the eighth month of the pregnancy, Mr and Mrs Morrison were told that Mrs Morrison was carrying twins. Having previously been told that there was only a single baby this came as an immense shock to them. This news coming so late in the day would be a shock to most people, but Mr and Mrs Morrison's expression of horror was extreme enough for the health visitor to get worried. However, she thought they would be able to manage as Mr Morrison had shown himself to be a good and caring father to Pamela. They said that it was actually fortunate that Mr Morrison was still unemployed as he would be available to help her.

At exactly the time Mrs Morrison came home from hospital with the new twins, Mr Morrison started some major adaptations in the house. He started to knock down walls, remove fireplaces and redecorate. Such was the major disruption he caused that the house started to resemble a building site. Mrs Morrison expressed some mild surprise that he should choose this particular time.

Pamela, previously an amenable toddler, suddenly became very demanding, seeking constant attention from her parents. At first the health visitor considered this a fairly normal reaction for a toddler displaced from being the only child and now having to cope with her jealousy of not one, but two, new babies. Her behaviour got worse and she refused to sleep at night. The sedation offered by the GP had no effect. Given a nursery place, she there showed herself to be the bright, energetic little girl she had previously been at home. She started to sleep again. However Mr Morrison was no longer the 'good' father. He was refusing to take his share of getting up in the night to the twins, as he had done with Pamela; and he was out all of every day working privately for various people, helping others, but doing nothing to help Mrs Morrison.

The health visitor became more alarmed when on her now more frequent visits she found Pamela feeding one of the twins and she was told of the special stodgy diet. The bickering between Mr and Mrs Morrison developed into bitter rows, and Pamela, who had been toilet trained before the birth of the twins, was now soiling in an angry and distressed way.

Things had gone badly wrong in this 'ideal' family. But why so badly wrong in *this* family (and some of the others in our sample)?

Mr Morrison had been perceived by his wife and the health visitor as a 'good' husband and father when he was in work. It seemed that he had been able to use the softer, caring side of his personality at home when his masculinity was secured and given expression at work. However he and Mrs Morrison had not been able to allow themselves to react in any distressed way when he lost his job; yet when they suffered a second shock, the news of the expected twins, they seemed to over-react. It was as if the impact of the loss of job had been completely denied and then only made itself felt when a second shock struck them.

The defensive process broke down and the reaction to the first loss, displaced on the second shock, doubled the impact of that shock and impaired their normal capacities. They continued to argue about Mr Morrison's refusal to help care for the new babies, but they never let themselves worry about his not finding work and providing for the family in a way they had been accustomed to when he brought in a well-above-average wage. In our discussions of this family we tended to refer to them as 'Mr and Mrs Twin-Shock'.

In the next chapter we describe other reactions to loss of job which we observed in our samples. We compare these reactions to what psychologists consider to be normal and healthy responses to experiences of different kinds of severe loss.

5

'Oh Absalom'

What! man; ne'r pull your hat upon your brows;
Give sorrow words; the grief that does not speak
Whispers the o'er fraught heart, and bids it break.'

Macbeth

My Mam used to say, 'Every tear shed in grief shortens the time
of a soul in purgatory.'

A widow from Balsall Heath

Like Shakespeare and the mother of the widow from Balsall
Heath, psychologists maintain that when there is loss, crisis,
bereavement, it is healthy to react to the reality of the
circumstances and experience the range of feeling normally
and uniquely associated with the event. When loss occurs, an
ability to grieve indicates mental health and an inner strength.
An inability to grieve indicates a weak ego with an
accompanying image that painful feelings can only destroy,
damage or send a person mad. There is evidence that people
who defend themselves from strong feelings of grief are often in
trouble later in their lives when a further loss rebounds on the
repressed feelings related to the first loss.[1] The double grief
then breaks the defensive barriers. Delayed or compounded
grief reactions can be quite overwhelming, out of proportion
and unduly persistent. They can result in severe physical
symptoms, mental breakdown or seriously impaired
functioning.

As we have seen from the description of Mr and Mrs
Morrison, their functioning as parents was seriously impaired
after a second shock when they failed to react or show any
distress after the first one of Mr Morrison's suddenly having
lost his job and all that meant to them. Apparently they did not
grieve after sustaining major losses. For both of them there

95

was the loss of income and financial self-sufficiency at a time when they were committed to a mortgage and were wanting to increase the size of their family. There was the loss of a regulated distance between them. Mr Morrison lost the means of exercising a particular skill which, it seemed, was to him an important expression of his masculinity. He also lost a ready made group which afforded him masculine company. He lost an image of himself. Mrs Morrison lost an image she held of her husband and probably of the pride she may have had in his work and his ability to bring home a good wage. That was the sort of man she had married. She joined in his denial of the losses and the seriousness of their situation. She, too, over-reacted when the doctor told her she was carrying twins. On the birth of the twins, she found herself losing the type of domestic and child-care support she had previously had and still expected from her husband.

Grief

Grief, a 'mental wound which heals slowly',[2] has been known about since time began. 'Would I had died for thee, Oh Absalom, my son, my son!' More formally introducing mourning as a normal function of the mind, Freud described the process in terms of the libido, previously invested in the lost, loved person, being gradually withdrawn and then redirected towards other living people. He likened the state of feeling to melancholia.[3] In 1872 Darwin observed facial expressions of typical adult grief and concluded they were a result of, on the one hand, a tendency to scream like a child, on the other, of the effort of the adult to suppress the scream.[4] More recent studies[5] of severe, but normal grief relating to untimely bereavement have been well documented and indicate that although 'the intensity of grief varies enormously from individual to individual ... there is none the less a basic overall pattern',[6] and that there are two distinct main stages in the normal grieving process.

The first stage consists of a welter of changing and conflicting emotions concerning both the person who is lost and the self who is left. In this stage the deceased is ever present in the thoughts of the bereaved and metaphorically is still much alive. In the second stage there is a gradual letting go of the lost person or, as we might say, he is allowed to die. Only then is there recovery and an ability to reinvest in new relationships.

Each stage can be divided into two phases. The first phase is that of numbness and disbelief – a state of shock, even if the death has been anticipated. This phase may last just a few hours, or stretch into days or even weeks. Disbelief is defensive and defences are tiring. Exhaustion and heavy sleep induces further numbness.

Secondly there is a phase of anguish and distress, at first making itself felt episodically before taking over more fully. The major characteristic of this phase is the conflict of emotions. Grief is invariably ambivalent. On the one hand there is the yearning for the lost person; at times a compulsive searching, catching a glimpse only to find, No, it was not him, not even really like him. As Parkes has stated, the 'perceptual set' of the mind is still derived from the previous experience of having been close to the lost person over time.[7] On the other hand, there is anxiety for the self:

> No one ever told me that grief felt like fear. I am not afraid, but the sensation is like being afraid. The same fluttering in the stomach, the same restlessness, the yawning. I keep on swallowing.[8]

And there is anger against the lost person. 'Oh, why did you leave me?' 'The frequency with which anger occurs as part of normal mourning has ... habitually been under-estimated. Yet all researchers have been struck by the regularity of its occurrence.'[9] And there is guilt for things said, or not said, while there was still time.

The mental pain from this conflict of emotions can literally hurt and physical symptoms are common. Nature is kind and a symptom which puts a person to bed allows the mental pain to be nursed and cossetted. Nature is also graphic and in identification with the lost person it is not unusual for a grief-stricken person to produce a symptom similar to that which killed the loved one. Pains in the heart are quite usual. The health record of the bereaved is, in fact, 'a good index of how a person is coping with the emotional problem of bereavement'.[10] The mental energy that is expended in this phase drains vitality and leaves the bereaved listless and with impaired powers of concentration.

> At other times it feels like being mildly drunk, or concussed. There is a sort of invisible blanket between the world and me. I find it hard to take in what anyone says. Or perhaps, hard to want to take it in. It is so uninteresting.[11]

Grief is lonely, yet the characteristic ambivalence can show itself in the shunning of company and other conflicted behaviour. Sleep is disturbed or hard to come by, thus further impairing normal mental functioning.

In the third phase of the total process, in the start of the letting go, the turbulent emotions recede and feelings of emptiness and despair, then depression take over. Depression is a more disorganised state of mind than despair. It feels not only sad, but, as the old 'perceptual set' is relinquished, unbearably chaotic. Relinquishment arouses anxiety and guilt, yet incurring, as it does, a review of the self, it holds the potential for change and allows room for the building of a new self-image. As psychoanalysts say, depression is its own healer.

In the fourth phase, the ego reassembles itself in an altered perceptual set and the bereaved find themselves free enough to start to relate anew to other people sometimes in ways different from before. In this period of reorganisation of the mind, vitality returns.

In this basic overall pattern, with one phase more predominant than another, the process is rarely linear; a new phase takes over only slowly with frequent regressions to earlier ones – back to the yearning or searching, or even back to the disbelief.

Grief can be delayed, inhibited or become chronic. People can get stuck in any of the first three phases. Those who cannot stand the turbulence of the second phase or the emptiness or chaotic feelings of the third may feel consciously or unconsciously that physically they will disintegrate as opposed to *deintegrate*. More defences may be needed and those of displacement or splitting may occur. The denial may persist or the helpless despair felt by most people for a period in the third phase may establish itself as a defence against the more chaotic feelings of depression which would normally follow. Despair, in contrast to depression, has a much firmer mental set, the subject finding blame for the present circumstances only in others, leaving him a continuously helpless victim at the mercy of external forces. Escape from this dull, hopeless and helpless despair is sometimes sought in compulsive and extreme action which in itself is destructive to the perpetrator.

The inability to move on and through the process of mourning seems to be related to the intensity of the feelings invoked, the strength of the ego and previous experiences of separation and loss and how they were encompassed. The earlier and more traumatic any previous losses have been, particularly if they occurred in early childhood when the ego was not developed enough to carry the mental pain, the more the impact of later losses will be defended.[12]

Since the research on bereavement by death there have been studies of the effects of other major, irretrievable losses, for example, the loss of limb by amputation.[13] The process of mourning is similar: first, shock; second, severe anxiety and distress, the phenomenon of the 'phantom limb' bearing much resemblance to the 'phantom husband' described by most widows; third, restlessness, apathy, hopelessness and depression – 'it was like grief, more or less';[14] fourth, reorganisation and redirection – varying degrees of adaptation to the changed circumstances of life. Again, it seems that those who allow themselves to be depressed eventually make a more appropriate adaptation, those unable to grieve and be actively depressed often show severe symptoms of tension months or years later.

All changed circumstances of life, not just those following unpredictable or untimely bereavement, injury or disaster of one form or another incur loss of continuity and of the familiar. And this is so, even when the change offers immense gains. Loss is part and parcel of life as we move through infancy, childhood, youth, middle and then old age. As has been said, 'All change invokes loss.' Being weaned, going off to school, leaving home, marrying, becoming a parent, the children's leaving home, retiring, all require the individual 'to restructure his way of looking at the world'[15] and of responding to the new way the world looks at him.

Whatever the advantages of the new situation, some of the

benefits of the previous one have to be relinquished whether it be a loss of a dependence or of an independence. One difference between loss from a major bereavement and this type of transitional or, as Erikson has called it, 'developmental loss',[16] is that the latter is predictable and happens to everyone. Even so, when people do not acknowledge this fact of life, they are often surprised that despite the pleasures of their new situation and it's being very much what they sought, they are sometimes moody or flat, irritable or emotionally volatile in their responses. Although much more subdued, the process of negotiating a new view of the self evokes a minor grief process and can be similarly defended against. Those who can allow themselves the recognition of loss as well as gain are those who eventually make a better adaptation. As Marris states:

> Whenever we impose disruptive change on ourselves or others, we need to allow some kind of moratorium on other business, so that people can give their minds to repairing the thread of continuity in their attachments; and we should not burden ourselves with so many simultaneous changes that our emotional resilience becomes exhausted. There is some evidence that an accumulation of personal changes, even if they are all desired, can provoke a breakdown in health.[17]

Even winning the pools can be quite disturbing and the bigger the win, the greater the disturbance.

Loss of job

Unemployment occasions many losses, particularly if the job was enjoyed, but also if not enjoyed but earning good money, bestowing status, ordering time and, most important of all, giving some meaning and purpose to a person's life through the transformation and symbolisation of the work experience. At its worst, and as an unpredicted loss, it can be traumatic and throw a person into a state of severe grief. At its best, perhaps chosen and not regretted, an adaptation to the new circumstances has to be encompassed, incurring some lesser grief *en route*.

Studies of the impact of unemployment on individuals and families were undertaken in the 1930s[18] and again in the last decade.[19] There is a similarity to the description of grief after bereavement in the charting of phases of reaction after loss of job: the phase of shock, despite previous rumours of the factory closing; a phase of denial of the implications and an unreal optimism even in areas where unemployment is extensive; a phase of anxiety, distress and anger when the reality of the situation impinges and the loss makes itself felt. It is then that the job which was lost may become idealised in retrospect – even unpleasant and disliked jobs. This may well be due to the latent functions of work and unconscious meaning of jobs described in Part I of this book; until a person gives up a job, or has a job taken from him, he may not know what that job has psychologically carried for him.

The fourth phase is sometimes called that of resignation and adjustment.[20] We think it should be called resignation *or* adjustment. There is a marked difference between those who pass through grief, perhaps a lesser grief, and make a creative adaptation, finding new satisfactions and meaning in their lives, and those who just resign themselves to the inevitable:

'I've got adapted but I don't want to adapt. You could easily stay like that. I could be on the dole for the rest of my life.'[21]

or

'The longer it goes on the more you get careless with yourself and about yourself.'[22]

This is hardly a creative adjustment.

As Hill has said:

Indeed, the unemployed often become uneasily aware that as time goes on they develop a kind of inertia that is psychologically debilitating. They feel insufficiently stimulated and undervalued. The terms they use to describe their condition include 'depression', 'boredom' and 'laziness'. They feel increasingly that they are becoming not only occupationally, but psychologically, deskilled. They are less able to search for work or to get back to it if a job were available.[23]

For 'depression' 'boredom' and 'laziness' we would translate *despair*.

Most follow-up studies on the impact of unemployment are

on immediate response and are completed within a year or two.
Much less is known about the long-term effects, but Hill
described the period nine months to a year after loss of job:

> There is a settling down to the life of unemployment. Habits
> stabilise. Active work ceases or takes place at a lower level. The
> individual adjusts to a domestic or economic routine consistent
> with chronic unemployment and develops various psychological
> defences.[24]

Our clients had been unemployed various lengths of time, some
only for a few months, others for years. The longest period of
unemployment in our sample was ten years. And those clients
described in the last chapter at the time they signalled for help
displayed various psychological defences brought into service
to protect them from one or other phase of their grief.

Mr Treacher and Mr and Mrs Streatfield were trying to
escape from a state of despair. Mr Treacher, feeling that
'everything was totally useless', with no sense of purpose and
meaning, tried to escape by the extreme action of taking an
overdose. Later, when even more affected by the threat of the
loss of his wife, he 'threw a wobbly' in the gynaecological ward.
Mr Streatfield escaped into male company and excessive
drinking, Mrs Streatfield to her parents. Mr Rowlands
remained despairing and helpless, unable to 'deal with
ordinary crises of life'.

Mr and Mrs Fairchild who had 'no problem' seemed to be
asking for a safe forum in which they could become more
depressed about their losses, their current situation and their
own behaviour. Offered a period of containment once a week
for three months, they moved through some depressing
feelings. This churned them up and 'like a visit to the dentist'
they found it painful; but they emerged at the end feeling
stronger and better able to manage the many difficulties which
still lay ahead for them.

When Mrs Bell came for the initial consultation at the IMS,
she clearly remembered the words of a marriage guidance
counsellor whom she had seen on one occasion after she had
left her first husband: 'You have spent your whole life running
out of difficult situations. If you don't stop now and look at
some of the problems in yourself, you will spend the rest of

your life doing the same thing.' These words had made a great impression on her, although then she did not accept the advice. Now things were so wrong in her second marriage, she decided she would heed it. However she soon started to get very depressed or despairing – we are not sure which – first retreating to bed with the covers over her head and unable to get herself to the Institute. And then she ran away from the IMS and from her husband. We can only assume that the degree of her depression or despair was too frightening.

Mr and Mrs Morrison never reacted to the loss of his job. He failed to move through the phase of denial. His optimism remained high despite the reality of the situation. A second shock broke the defensive barrier and the expectations of twins had to carry all the shock, some of it displaced from the earlier one of the loss of job. Then further defensive processes took over – a leap into intense activity of house alteration which was inappropriate in its timing just when the twins were coming home from hospital. When this failed to serve, his anger came more to the fore but was expressed indirectly and passively in his refusal to support and help Mrs Morrison in the care of the children. As she became more tired, more distressed and more angry with him, the rows became serious. They railed and hit out at each other rather than at the economic and industrial forces which had deprived him of a job. It seemed they would soon be heading for divorce.

This is not unusual. The divorce statistics for 1983 show that 'overall the rate was highest for unemployed husbands (who it might be suspected were disproportionately drawn from the unskilled). For each age group the divorce rate for the unemployed was about double that of the national average.[25]

In a recent paper,[26] Haskey, in examining the social and demographic characteristics of couples who divorced on different grounds between 1979 and 1981, stated:

> The distribution by fact proven of decrees granted to wives of unemployed husbands is distinctive. If the relative frequencies of proving the different facts can be taken as a true measure of the likelihood of occurrence of each of the different situations they describe, it may be concluded that *unemployed husbands who are divorced by their wives more often have behaved in an intolerable manner*, [our italics] compared to the average

husband divorced by his wife, but are only half as likely to have committed adultery.

This pattern is similar to that for husbands in Social Class V, from whom a disproportionate number of unemployed husbands might be expected to be drawn, and also to that for economically inactive husbands, a broader group which includes the unemployed. Apparently Mr Morrison, previously perceived by the health visitor as an 'ideal' husband and father, is one of many whose behaviour became intolerable.

And the social worker who spoke of being 'stuck in the illness model' was no exception. In their recently published longitudinal study of family health undertaken before and after a meat factory closed in Calne, Wiltshire, Beale and Nethercote[27] found a 20% increase in consultation of a GP, a 20% increase of referral to a specialist and a 60% increase in hospital outpatient attendance. This study period covered six years of continuous employment, the workers under threat of factory closure for the last two of these years, and two years after closure – eight years in all. Two findings are of particular importance.

First, 'No significant differences were found when testing years five and six against years seven and eight'. The difference was between years four and five. The threat of redundancy was 'a stress equal to, if not greater than, the actual event'.

Secondly, although the number of consultations rose by 20%, the number of new illnesses increased by only 11%. The 'families either developed an increased doctor dependency or the symptoms with which they presented proved more difficult to diagnose and treat. It is possible that their problems were less clear cut, their distress more psychosomatic in type or their disorders less responsive to simple measures.'

As mentioned in the last chapter, Beale and Nethercote also commented on 'the reluctance of the unemployed to admit to their predicament'. Shame is yet one more feeling to be added to the mixture of emotions. 'Fourteen per cent of the workforce in Britain', they continue, 'are now suffering, together with their families, from what might correctly be called an epidemic, and only for a small minority is that fact recorded in their notes.' If, as Bowlby said, the health record is a good index of how a person is coping with the emotional problems of bereavement, this 14% are still grieving or defending themselves from their grief.

Recent studies of suicide and deliberate self harm (parasuicide) have shown an over-representation of unemployed people compared with the general population.[28] A notable finding of Platt and Kreitman[29] was 'the role of long-term unemployment. After one year the risk approached double that for shorter periods.'

Chronic grief

The picture described in these studies is a gloomy one and seems gloomier than that of bereavement by death when it seems that however deep the anguish, often lasting months, many people move through the mental pain and find hope and pleasure in a newly constructed life. This does not mean that they do not carry a scar and that they do not have moments or periods of intense sadness. We may know of some people, much fewer in number, who have broken down or remained stuck in their grief, still enshrining a lost person and unable to find compensatory interests or invest in a new relationship.

We may also know some people who still carry a scar from a long period of unemployment in the 1930s, either their own or that of a parent – a persistent insecurity as to where the bread is coming from, despite a subsequent, adequate pay packet. We probably know others who have been recently unemployed and seem their old selves once they are back and feeling safely back in employment. And we know people who say their redundancy 'made them', forcing them into a new type of job or a new way of life which they eventually found more satisfying. However, they often comment on the stress they experienced during the process of re-establishing themselves.

We are concerned with those who have not got back into paid employment and have not made a creative adaptation – the casualties who have failed to move through their grief and remained deeply distressed or despairing. Studies of the 1930s and the 1970s describe some devastating impacts of unemployment and changes in family structure following it.[30] In Chapter 7 we describe some of the effects and changes in marital structure we observed in our sample. Yet the question

remains, Is bereavement from loss of work as devastating or
more devastating to some people than bereavement from death
of a loved one, in that so many – too many – unemployed people
fail to recover and adjust other than by finding a job? At
present such jobs are hard to find in some areas of the country.

No one can answer that question for another and many
people may have no basis for comparison. For some people it
may be true – the meaning of work is more important to them
than the meaning of love in the maintenance of their sense of
identity. We suggest, however, that the amount of chronic grief
described in all the studies of unemployment is due to several
factors, only some of them relating to the intensity of the grief.
Others relate to the process of mourning after loss of job. Our
evidence suggests that the *process of mourning may be more
complex and more difficult to encompass after loss of a job than
after loss of a loved one*. We outline six psychological factors –
three relating to the actual grief, three to the mourning process
– which we believe account for the intensity of grief and the
complexity of the mourning process after loss of job.

Intensity of grief

The weight of keystones

Freud, as quoted in Chapter 1, placed love *and* work as the two
main keystones of life, implying they might have roughly equal
weight. Klein, writing in the 1930s, saw these two keystones
'forever linked' in the unconscious, because of the infant's
experiencing food and love coming from the same source.

> Security was first afforded to us by our mother, who not only
> stilled the pangs of hunger, but also satisfied our emotional
> needs and relieved anxiety. Security attained by satisfaction of
> our essential requirements is, therefore, linked with emotional
> security.[31]

By the same token, threat to obtaining livelihood and self-
preservation can be felt as loss of love. This linkage gives
additional meaning to the idea of work as 'the acceptable
mistress', when, as we noted in Chapter 3, it is substituted for
love.

However, as Marris has stated, 'Love does not explain grief. The fundamental crisis of bereavement arises, not from loss of others, but from *loss of self* [our italics]'.[32] Familiar habits of thought and behaviour no longer make sense. He quoted characteristic phrases of widows which 'seemed to express more than simple apathy':

'I lost all interest.'
'I went dead.'
'When the bottom falls out of your life.'
'I had nothing to live for.'

He continued:

These words imply more than loss of a relationship, however important. Everything has gone – as if bereavement had destroyed them, and they were mourning their own death. When the dead person has been, as it were, the keystone of a life, the whole structure of meaning in that life collapses when the keystone falls. ... When a widow says life has no meaning any more, she is expressing a literal truth, for the relationship which principally defined who she was and what she had to do is gone. This is true of an unhappy marriage as well as a happy one, so long as she had not already begun to extricate herself from it. The intensity of grief is related to the intensity of involvement, rather than of love.

Marris might have written differently if his study had been on widowers. We think there is a difference between men and women (although with numerous exceptions and various shadings in between) as to whether the greater intensity of involvement is in respect of relationships or employment. As we indicated in Chapter 3, the paid employment of the majority of women accommodates their husband's job and domestic and child care concerns. Employed or not employed outside the home, they are more likely to define their identity through the making of relationships and the child-bearing and caring role. The caring role is a major part of their work. This may be why they tend to be less satisfied with marriage than men as reflected in their more often being the divorce petitioners. In Bernard's terms,[33] *her* experience of marriage may be less satisfactory than *his* experience in the light of expectations of intensity of involvement in it. And when they are widowed, they lose their loved one *and* their work.

In contrast, for some men the consistent strand of employment may well be, in the intensity of involvement, the weightiest keystone, not only if loving intimacy is problematic for them, but also if, in Klein's terms, self-preservation and love are inextricably linked at an unconscious level and they are the main earner for the family. Apparently this was the case for some of our male clients. The whole structure of meaning in their life had collapsed. Such was the intensity of their attachment to work, they were mourning what seemed like their own death. As Mr Chester said, 'I felt dead inside.' Mrs Chester, identifying with him, added, 'We both felt dead inside.'

Intensity of ambivalence

For other clients in our sample, work did not appear to be the main keystone of their life and yet they were also feeling 'dead inside' and failing to negotiate the normal course of mourning. Studies on grief, while indicating that intensity does not depend on the strength of the love, do suggest that the intensity is greater and the process of mourning more difficult to encompass when the feelings for the deceased person are highly ambivalent.[34] Some of our clients had poor work records and were among the first to lose their jobs when a firm was retracting. Clearly they had been ambivalent either about having to work or about a particular job.

Seabrook[35] emphasises the differences between what has been lost in the redundancies of the 1970s and what was lost in those of the 1930s. Then the lost work had often been relentless and hard and

> an affront to intelligence. But there were two great consolations: the sense of the indispensability of their labour in occupations that were plainly essential, however poorly rewarded, and a sense of a shared predicament. ... Unemployment in that atmosphere had a particular pain.

But, as he says of the 1970s,

> ... as labour has become detached from products and services that are directly identifiable with perceived human need, its whole concept is transformed. The idea of redundancy has a

resonance now that goes far beyond the lay-off of workpeople in a given industry.

We may wonder how redundant some of our clients felt even before they were laid off if they could not relate the limited automatic task they had to perform to the final product, or if they could not use their jobs to lay old ghosts to rest. In these circumstances, their ambivalence would intensify their grief.

When Mr and Mrs Walton first sought help for their sexual problem, Mr Walton had not lost his job, but with the rest of the workforce had heard the general threat that there might be some redundancies. He had become increasingly withdrawn from Mrs Walton and in her panic to reduce the distance between them, she became more controlling but had also 'gone off sex'. In view of Mr Walton's skilled trade and possibility of obtaining alternative employment, his despair and anxiety seemed beyond what the circumstances warranted. The counsellor described him as 'meek and unable to say "Boo to a goose"'. However his ambivalence about his job seemed relevant to his level of distress. He had recently been promoted from an outside job which he did well to an inside job behind a desk. Despite his initial pride in his promotion, he now did not feel a man, he said, 'just inadequate'. In addition, he had as a boy defied his parents in his choice of job. They had wanted him to follow in his father's footsteps and eventually take over the family business. He had need to escape from his powerful mother who ruled the roost, but now he was afraid she would say, 'I told you so.'

Intensity of shame

Earlier in this chapter we quoted Beale and Nethercote on 'the reluctance of the unemployed to admit to their predicament', and we commented on the shame associated with unemployment. Despite death being a fact of life and everyone expecting to be bereaved at some time or other, feelings of shame are not unusual in the process of mourning. They form part of the uncomfortable mixture of feelings, particularly when associates are awkward in the presence of the grief of the bereaved. After loss of job, however, shame appears to be much more intense, presumably because so many of the unemployed have grown up with a work ethic and have never expected to be out of work until what used to be considered a normal age for retirement.

Shame is defined in the *Concise Oxford Dictionary* as 'a feeling of humiliation excited by consciousness of (especially one's own) guilt or shortcoming, of having made oneself or been made ridiculous, or of having offended against propriety, modesty or decency'. People describing their own sense of shame usually refer to a conviction that they are inferior or defective, defining themselves as no good or not good enough. Miller,[36] a psychologist, studying shame, stressed the 'displeasure about the status of the self – of having no significance'. She said:

> The rhythmic experience of shame ... is the characteristic experience of shrinking away from others and pulling inward and downward. ... The centre of the self is diminished and the shamed want to disappear or to hide.

Many of the clients in our samples also found it difficult to 'admit to their predicament'. Mr Astor who became unemployed during the course of the marital therapy, continued to maintain that he was working as a self-employed consultant, although there was no evidence that he had acquired any work. He and others appeared literally smaller in size than when in work, pulled 'inward and downward'. Many were reduced to shadows of their former selves. In Chapter 7 we describe this phenomenon in which curtains were kept drawn and door bells left unanswered.

Miller also spoke of the loss of dignity and loss of power which are crucial elements of humiliation:

> Rage is often felt, but only as impotent rage. ... Shame is an experience that grows with unnatural vigour when aggression cannot be used to counteract it.

The rage related to what is often seen to be man-made unemployment is impotent. Despite the number (just above three million at the point of going to press) in this situation, they constitute a small, poor and largely unskilled minority, cut off from the mainstream of British society. (A society in which between 1976 and 1982 the rich got richer and the poor got poorer; the spending capacity of workers increased, and the spending capacity of the unemployed decreased: 'Social Trends show that income disparities both as between the skilled and the unskilled in employment and among households in the country as a whole, have widened since the mid-1970s. ... The top fifth of households increased their share of post tax income from 37.9% to 39.4% and the bottom fifth slipped from 7.4% to 6.9%.')[37]

The unemployed lack numerical power to rebel. Their anger remains impotent, and the intensity of their grief is multiplied as the 'shame grows with natural vigour'.

Complexity of mourning

Keeping sane: 9.00 a.m. – 5.00 p.m.

After bereavement from death of a loved one, work and its structure are often used as a prop, a means of getting through the day. It provides some containment for the distress or some temporary relief from it. Concentration may at first be poor and employers may not get good value, but the bereaved have to get up, go out and try to apply themselves to a task which has meaning beyond their immediate concerns. They remain connected to the world beyond their family. 'The thing which helped me most when my husband died was getting a job' is a typical comment quoted in several studies on bereavement.

Mrs Philpot was in paid employment when she and her husband suffered a severe personal loss. 'My work kept me sane,' she said. Some years later she suffered another personal loss which entailed her leaving her job. When she was able to work again, she failed to find another post. At the time she was referred to a practitioner, her excessively made-up face remained a mask showing no glimmer of feeling. Like a zombie, she told how she managed the domestic chores, feeding and cleaning for her husband and children. For herself, she said, she 'had no hope', and then corrected this to 'one hope' – if she could find a job, she would at least feel 'partially alive'.

Mrs Young, a widow, presented at the pilot workshop and not in our sample of married clients, suffered a series of mental breakdowns. With regular counselling help from a social worker, she always managed to get back on her feet and into a job. To get back into work was her strongest motive in aiding her recovery. She was an isolated person with few friends and relatives. Work, rather than love, was her keystone of life. A job helped her to feel part of the world. After her last breakdown and with the worsening unemployment situation, she failed to get a job. And the social worker gave up hope that she would get one. Without her own and his hope, she quietly committed suicide. The social worker blamed himself for *his* loss of hope.

If a job, as a keystone of life, is a means of keeping sane when untimely and traumatic loss plunges a person into a state of grief, the non-existence of that prop just because it is the object of loss is clearly going to make the process of mourning more difficult to encompass than it would otherwise be. We think this may be one of the main reasons why so many redundant workers fail to complete the mourning process. The love relationship and domestic sphere, the other main keystone of life, may not be as containing an environment in terms of regular and ordered structure, of linkage to a purpose beyond the self, and of offering relief from the mixture of feelings. Without work and going out to work, people are thrown back on themselves and the resources of their immediate family with reduced finances and, therefore, less means with which to distance themselves occasionally. The other adult in that family situation is the partner who is also affected in many ways. Also shocked, also having to change her lifestyle, her resource may well be not as sustaining as that of a group of non-grieving workmates.

Married grief

In situations of grief, there is usually a chief mourner who is offered condolence and support. In our sample, the one who had lost the job would be assumed to be the chief mourner and have the love and support of his partner. Certainly some of our clients had received this. Mr and Mrs Fairchild were closer in their marriage after his employment than they had ever been before through her support of him. Mrs Chester felt very exploited after Mr Chester had chased a job in the Middle East and there fallen in love with another woman 'after all she had done for him' when he was unemployed; and worse, it was her idea in the first place that he should apply for this job. When he left home to give the job a trial before the whole family moved, she had had difficulty in not showing her jealousy of his escape from the strained domestic scene.

However, it was not so with many of our clients. As Mr Walton withdrew from his wife, she attempted to heighten her control over him. This was unproductive, as it drove him further in on himself. Mrs Streatfield may previously have been a castrating wife, but, as we may guess, in her anxiety she probably became even more so when he was unemployed.

Obviously the wives were deeply affected by their partner's loss of job, particularly by the loss of income and of the standard of living they had come to expect. Some of them had also lost the man they had married and become used to if, in his bereaved state, his behaviour radically changed. Mrs Morrison, for example, lost the help and support she had previously from Mr Morrison in the care of one baby. Then with three babies, she needed his support even more, but lost his actual help and also the image of herself married to a husband who was a good and caring father.

Mrs Holloway loved her husband because he was 'a brick wall'. Unlike her parents, he was reliable. When Mr Holloway was made redundant, losing the symbol of his father's love, he became anxious and edgy, and then very passive, staying in bed long hours, watching TV and going out only to exercise the dog. Sex stopped. Mrs Holloway became increasingly unhappy and confused and felt her 'brick wall' had deserted her.

Another group of clients seemed to be more affected by the loss of their partner's actual job than by his changed behaviour, particularly if his behavour was not as immobilised or as intolerable as that of some others. The status of that job or the 'trappings of power' had clearly been a major keystone of their own self-image. This surprised us when the wife held a job worthy of comparable esteem. Sometimes being 'at the top', or apparently on the way to the top, was an important factor. Mrs Carter had divorced one husband, and was seriously considering divorcing the next one, when the first and then the second failed to achieve her aspirations for them.

The second already shaky marriage started to falter when Mr Carter gave up one job which entailed a foreign posting. He had queried how they would manage with a young baby in a strange culture where she would be unlikely to be able to find a job for herself and when she was already showing difficulty in adjusting to the role of unpaid mother. He used the opportunity to start his own business, but the speed with which he moved did not satisfy her and the marriage deteriorated even further.

Loss of limelight was a factor for some. Mr and Mrs Bell made a conscious decision that he would change his job and life-style when they married, as they both desperately wanted a 'normal' family life. Yet she was quite clear that she had initially been attracted by the worldly wise man who had played the saxophone to applauding audiences in all the major cities of the world. She had applauded too. Married and running his own business, he was less confident, less worldly wise, and, in her estimation, totally incompetent. Clearly they both suffered the lack of applause.

In situations in which the wife had lost either the man she thought she had married or the indirect narcissistic satisfaction which his job had given her, there were *two chief mourners*. Although we do not know of a study which has looked at this in detail, our experience in the IMS suggests that grief is sometimes more difficult to handle when there are two chief mourners than when there is only one. For example, when a couple lose a child, they probably expect help and comfort from each other and feel bitterly let down – betrayal is probably not too strong a word – when their equally grief-stricken partner is not able to give them this. Grief can bring people closer together. It can also drive them apart, particularly if, in its intensity and characteristic ambivalence, opposing defences are brought into operation.

In Chapter 3, we explained how a conflict can get externalised between the partners, each of them carrying one set of feelings, not only for themselves, but for the partner as well. In shared grief, it can happen that one partner carries all the sadness, the other all the anger. If there is a need to split the feelings and keep one set unconscious, the expression of it by the partner may feel intolerable: 'Why is she so angry? It wasn't the doctor's fault – anyway, anger won't bring him back.' 'Why does he just mope? I can't bear his tears.'

As we explained in Chapter 3, people who consistently and

inflexibly use the defence of projection to deal with one of their conflicting emotions seem to choose a marriage partner who employs a similar defensive procedure. In her castrating behaviour, Mrs Streatfield seemed to be expressing her own and Mr Streatfield's anger about his not being in work; he sitting slumped in the chair, was expressing the dull, sad, lethargic and 'stupid' despair for them both.

The unclosed system

'Anyway, anger won't bring him back' – nor will any amount of searching. The third phase of the mourning process constitutes a slow acceptance of the inevitable: death is final; the loved person will not return; there is only dust or ashes. The old perceptual set is gradually relinquished allowing space for a new self-image to be established.

One of the problems for unemployed people is that intellectually they do not know whether their redundancy is final or not. Should they strive to adjust; or should they go on searching for employment if they have the energy to do so? It is as if many of them remain suspended in their grief, almost hopeless and yet not quite able to give up the hope. They receive contrary economic and political messages: the recession is temporary, industry will recover, jobs are now available, get on your bike and search; or technological change means that there will never be enough jobs, society is moving into a post-industrial phase. In this social climate, are the unemployed supposed to move through their grief and adjust, or should they remain in a state of temporary suspension with even greater despair and sense of helplessness engendered by the conflicting messages? Mr Streatfield did his six-months stint in the day centre and was taught a fancy skill for which there was no opening in the world of paid work. Others of our clients in the Tyneside area had become much excited when they read in the paper of a new industrial development being brought into the town. They relapsed into their despair when skilled labour was imported from the south.

The social psychological context

These six psychological factors which we believe account for

the intensity of the grief and the complexity of the mourning
process after loss of job need to be placed in their wider social
context.

Unemployment in the 1970s and 1980s followed a period
with an unprecedentedly high employment rate. (From 1950 to
1969 the mean unemployment rate was 1.8% with a stable
average of 2%.) This was a period of relative affluence when
wages kept pace with rising prices. Our samples, like the rest
of the adult unemployed population, grew up or spent the first
half of their working life in this economic and social climate.
Their expectations of work and of level of remuneration were
fashioned by it. Work and financial independence were taken
for granted.

During this time work in industry became more automated
and less obviously indispensable. On the other hand, creature
comforts became more indispensable and the drive for their
acquisition was fuelled by the pressure of increased marketing
skills, in particular of psychologically sophisticated adver-
tisements flashed repeatedly on the television screen into the
living room.

We again quote Seabrook, comparing the pressures of work
with the pressures of acquisition:

> If the pressure of relentless work prevented millions from
> developing their real powers and abilities, the changed and
> easier conditions, instead of releasing them, demand less and
> less of working people and just as effectively inhibit and lock up
> their strengths and abilities as poverty ever did ... They have
> been nurtured in a closed world of material things brought to
> perfection, goods that cry their competitive desirability at them
> from the moment they were born. Their only business, it seems,
> is to yearn and strive for possession of them. In this way the
> primary determinant of their lives has been, not work, not doing
> or contributing anything, but on the lopsided insistence of
> buying, getting and having.[38]

In the 1930s many people were proud of how well they
managed on very little. As Illich has said, 'Expectations grow
while hopeful trust in one's own competence declines.'[39]

Competence declines with reduced resources. To be
unemployed in Britain for the majority is to be poor. (In 1981 it
was estimated that just over 2.6 million unemployed people

and members of their families were living in poverty or at its margin.[40] The longer the period of unemployment, with savings expired and the subsequent inability to replace household goods and personal belongings, the poorer the poor become and the more visible their poverty. (The long-term rate of supplementary benefit is not paid to unemployed people after one year on benefit.)

The problem of attempting to trace the interaction of the economic and psychological effects of unemployment are so complex that few attempts have been made to do this. However, Jahoda and her colleagues in their famous study of Marienthal in the 1930s noted a connection between the ability to cope and the level of household income. They concluded that a psychological deterioration ran 'parallel to the narrowing of economic resources and the wear and tear of personal belongings'.[41]

'Poverty is not only about shortage of money. It is about rights and relationships, about how people are treated.'[42] As Donnison has stated, 'The first thing which poor people are deprived of is power. That's why they get consigned to the places and roles which no one else wants to occupy.'[43] Actual poverty is made worse by relative poverty. 'In recent years social welfare and taxation policies have tended to benefit the rich at the expense of the poor.'[44] The rich have got richer and the poor have got poorer. The majority of people who are in employment are better off in material terms now than they were ten or fifteen years ago.[45] Income from employment has risen from some £30 billion in 1970 to some £170 billion (equivalent to £37 billion in terms of 1970 purchasing power) in 1983. Increasing the divide, the proportion of all workers on overtime has remained remarkably steady, but in manufacturing industries has actually increased from 1981 to 1983. When jobs are short, family and informal networks are one of the more successful means of finding unskilled work; fathers get sons jobs, and sons get their fathers jobs. Many families have several earners. (Employed male heads of households are nearly twice as likely as unemployed male heads to have working wives [probably because of the consequent loss of welfare benefits].[46])

Poverty, actual and relative, is linked to the standard of housing; 'poor people live in poor houses':[47] poor in terms of the

architectural disasters of the 1960s – the forest of bland tower
blocks looming above 'an eerie wasteland of unkempt grass',[48]
with the accompanying isolation for families with children;
poor in terms of serious design faults in previously untried
building systems; poor in terms of inadequate maintenance
which now affects much council and privately rented
accommodation, as the best stock gets sold off and
home-ownership so favoured by the employed remains beyond
the reach of the unemployed. As suburban factories have
closed or contracted, overspill estates have become more
deprived than some inner city areas, 'forgotten areas of
deprivation, displaced fragments of inner city decline';[49] the
majority of inhabitants are cut off from employment
opportunities, utterly dependent on state benefits and,
therefore, without the means to generate an informal economy
of home maintenance and local services.[50] Many of the clients
on our workshop sample, particularly in the Tyneside area,
were surrounded by the despair and apathy of their
neighbours.

Housing is of greater signifance in a poor climate. A bad
winter increases the stress and distress of poverty and
unemployment, not only in terms of cold and inability to buy
more clothes and blankets or pay fuel bills, but also in keeping
the family indoors. (Two of the families in our workshop
sample had moved from Tyneside to Devon partly because of
the weather, but in doing so had deprived themselves of a close
social network.) But even in Devon the weather was not always
kind and, as for those in Tyneside, winter meant even longer
hours in front of 'the killer of time'[51] and 'even sicker at seeing
himself doing it'.[52]

Television, as well as being a constant and painful reminder
of the opportunities of a consumer society beyond the reach of
the unemployed, is also a disseminator of news. Rapid social
change constitutes news, and when the overall unemployment
figure rose from 6.8% in 1980 to 10.5% in 1981 and 12.2% in
1982, unemployment became news. Diagrams brought the
figures alive and maps pinpointed the location of large factory
closures and the opening of smaller ones many miles away.
Using Flaim's term, 'the discouraged worker'[53] (the unemployed individual who sees himself as so unlikely to find work
that he withdraws himself from the labour market altogether),

Kelvin and Jarrett, commenting on the social shaping of the perception of the unemployed person, thought this to be one source of the discouragement.

Another source of discouragement is how the unemployed are treated not just by the policy makers, but also by the employed. 'Frequently they feel they are treated as second-class citizens', by the level of provision, the conditions for obtaining welfare benefit 'involving invasions of privacy ... which would be deemed intolerable in relation to "ordinary" men and women'.[54]

The grief responses to unemployment of the clients in our samples were partly shaped by their personalities and partly by the stress invoked by these economic and social realities we have described. Three factors always need to be included in the 'equation of person-environment fit: the objective social environment; the individual's perception of that environment related to his personal characteristics; and finally the physiological, affective and behavioural reactions which act in mediation'[55] or, as we add, *in accentuation*. For example, as we noted earlier in this chapter, health records are an indicator of how a person is coping with grief and stress. Illness causes further stress. Yet the Archbishop's report on the deprivation in Urban Priority Areas (with unemployment being one of the six indicators of deprivation) showed that people in these areas were not only less healthy, but also less well cared for than in non-deprived areas. The figures show the stark geography of the likelihood of dying tomorrow – far higher in Gateshead and Newcastle than in, for example, Scarborough or Harrogate. 'Statistics of mortality and morbidity are quite literally indicators of life chances.'[56]

Much of the research into the relationship between mental health and environment fails to come up with clear associations, and the results of one study are often contradicted by another.[57] There are, however, two conclusions that can be drawn. First, that in such a highly complex subject, both individual and environmental factors must be regarded as equally important.[58] Secondly, that mental health is related not so much to the environment in its physical structural sense, but more to the social processes connected to that setting. In their turn, these processes are determined not only by the structure of the environment, but also by the culture, economy and political ideology which govern it.[59]

Kelvin and Jarrett emphasise the fact that although there is a 'clear consensus of evidence that in the great majority of cases prolonged unemployment leads to resignation and apathy', and the 'ultimate position may be the same for all,' this does not 'entail that they all got there the same way: the levelling of individual differences in resignation and apathy is significant precisely because the starting points and intermediate stages will so often have been different.'[60]

We have described the various 'stages' in which we observed our clients in a process of a complex mourning of an intense loss, usually stuck in one stage or another, thereby exercising a defence against the continuing process. We believe the degree of intensity of the loss of job is accounted for by personal characteristics and the meaning of the job for a particular individual, and by social factors which emphasise the value of work and increase the stress of unemployment; and that the complexity of negotiating a normal mourning process is similarly heightened by personal, marital and social factors.

We remind the reader that the ability to move through the process of mourning depends on the intensity of the loss *and* the strength of the ego to handle the mixture of opposing feelings. We believe that in the economic and social climate we have described the ego needs the strength of an ox; and that many people who would otherwise bear their grief and come to terms with a new view of themselves and a new way of life become psychological casualties when beset by loss of the opportunity to work with its attendant disadvantages – probably the most important being the loss of power and loss of life chances.

We also mentioned earlier in this chapter that the ability to mourn depended on previous experiences of loss and how that was handled. Many of the clients in our samples had suffered severe losses earlier in their lives and were particularly vulnerable to further loss. They could be categorised as an already deprived group, their starting point heavily handicapped. In the next chapter we describe what happened to them when the loss of job reactivated the feelings associated with these earlier losses which had not been properly grieved.

6

Reverberations

Everlasting farewells! and again, and yet again reverberated –
everlasting farewells!

De Quincey

Early deprivation

We do not know the life stories of all the clients in our samples;
but we know many of them and the sad list of lack of love or
loss of love in childhood suggests that as a group they would be
particularly vulnerable to major losses later in their lives.

Someone sure of his own worth, brought up knowing that he
was loved and cherished for his own sake, is less likely than the
already deprived to feel totally destroyed when told that he is
redundant. He may at first be disbelieving, then shaken, even
shocked to his core, and subsequently disorientated, angry,
anxious and depressed as he faces up to the number of losses
that are incurred. His resources may well be weakened by the
factors which make the mourning process after loss of job so
complex as mentioned in the last chapter. He may feel a keen
sense of injustice, but his inner core of worth and belief in
himself will sustain him through his grief and keep him in
touch with the economic circumstances so that the blow is not
felt just in personal terms.

We are talking of a confidence in the self which will allow
that basically strong self to be shaken and to feel the impact of
the blow; and also of an innate optimism and resourcefulness
born of the early experience of physical and emotional security.
He will need, in Marris' terms, 'a moratorium' – a breathing
space to grieve the losses and to 'repair the thread of his own
continuity'. He will need to come to terms with a new view of
himself, no longer the man who never expected to be out of a

job. Yet, with this inner resource, he is the person more likely to be able to adjust to and make the most of a life-style of non-paid work, or 'to get on his bike', even if he has to borrow it first, and, when searching for work among fierce competition, he is the person more likely to convince a prospective employer that he is the man to take on.

In contrast, we can imagine the reverberation of the word *redundant* in the mind of Mr Quigley who thought he

> had never been wanted as a child because he had been born a boy.

Feeling redundant, as it were, from the start, redundancy from work is yet a further confirmation of the image of worthlessness and not being wanted. And in accordance with Melanie Klein's idea that threat to livelihood is felt as loss of love, the deprived, feeling even less lovable than usual, are likely to be either in a deeper state of despair than previously or even more defended against the underlying feeling of hopelessness which the seriously deprived often fight against all their lives.

Mr Quigley's counsellor was struck by his degree of panic when he first came to see her. His degree of distress had persuaded the appointments clerk to arrange for him to be seen there and then. The immediate crisis was that his wife had been rushed to hospital and he was left to care for the other two young children. He was unemployed, he said, depressed, and unable to face the prospect of caring for these children. He was angry because he had not wanted this pregnancy anyhow, and now his wife was getting all the support in hospital and he was getting none at home. His family lived locally but were refusing to help out. His mother had said, 'It's your family, you made the decision to marry, they are your children, and you get on and look after them.'

Even at this stage of the counselling, his envy of his wife – the one who got cared for – so characteristic of people who have always felt unloved, came through clearly. Quite apart from the immediate rejection he experienced from his mother, it was obviously unbearable for him at a deeper level that he, so uncared for, was left to be the carer of the children while his wife, as he imagined, was the one who was getting looked after.

At the next meeting he was less angry with her as he no longer saw her as the one getting all the attention. She was feeling 'depersonalised', she had told him, because the hospital was more interested in the pregnancy than in her.

Like many people who have always felt basically deprived of love, he could not give up the yearning for what he felt he had never had. In a very confused statement he talked about his mother. Despite her current refusal to help, he said he felt close to her and would like 'to dump the rest of the family and have her just for himself'. She was well educated, he said with pride, and had married beneath herself. As a child he had been seen as backward, but really he had been just bored. She should have understood this, he complained; but he just wanted her for himself, he said again with a whine in his voice, as he tried to make her into the mother he had wanted and still wanted her to be.

Mr and Mrs Quigley had a marital problem before his unemployment and before the latest pregnancy. It was a 'problem of communication', he said. He had married her because she believed in him and was better educated (like his mother in relation to his father). It had been her decision to have children and she had insisted on starting a family. Eventually he had given in to her wishes on the understanding that the children would be her sole responsibility. Feeling so uncared for, he clearly stated his lack of capacity to care. He wanted his wife, like his mother, just for himself.

Our clients were particularly vulnerable in their shared grief. As we explained in Chapter 3, shared anxieties, fantasies and defences are inherent in the unconscious choice of partner; despite the different images the partners might carry in their minds about what had gone wrong for them personally, a common concern, either conscious or unconscious, about deprivation would have been one factor in their initial attraction for each other and in their subsequent interaction. Mrs Quigley was equally beset with envy. While Mr Quigley could not bear the thought of her being fussed over by the nurses, apparently she perceived the staff paying more attention to the baby she carried than to herself.

The life histories of the wives echoed the deprivation of the husbands:

Adopted, rejected by adoptive parents; fostered, rejected by foster parents.

The picture of a seven-year-old doing the family ironing made a great impression on us. Mrs Bell said it was difficult to talk about her family. 'Things happened,' she said, 'between her father and herself.' He picked on her, the oldest girl. Her mother went out to work in the evenings and she was expected to look after the younger children. Twice he sexually assaulted her. Her mother never protected her because 'he would then take it out on the other children'. She remembered overhearing her mother say to her father, 'That girl has enough on you to put you away.' From the age of seven she wanted to leave home when she burnt herself on the iron. 'Yes, she did all the ironing.'

Several of the wives had, like Mrs Bell, been forced into being over-responsible as children. Mrs Todd's father had been an alcoholic and she, as the second eldest of ten children, had had to help her competent mother manage the family. Mrs Stokes had also been a capable girl. The eldest in her family, as far back as she could remember she periodically took over when her mother went into the mental hospital. Her grandmother who had helped out died when she was 14.

The efficiency of Mrs Bell and Mrs Stokes finally broke down when their husbands' unemployment and subsequent inability to provide for them (unconsciously to love them) as they wanted and needed reactivated old feelings that men (fathers) abused women and left them to do it all. The defensive barrier against the old griefs broke. Mrs Stokes threatened to throw herself and the two children off Tower Bridge and Mrs Bell just retreated under the bed clothes and then deserted her husband and children.

Mrs Todd did not lose her ability, but as her image of men as irresponsible beings was buttressed by her husband's unemployment, she became more and more resentful and even more over-employed, taking on seasonal jobs to help ends meet, but unable to encourage her husband to share the domestic duties.

Images of fathers, or relationships or lack of relationships with them were of particular importance in helping us to understand some of the extremely distressed reactions of some couples in our samples to the loss of the husband's job. This is not surprising in a culture in which over generations man's capacity to love and care is partially expressed and expected to be expressed in his ability to provide.

As described in Chapter 2, some of the husbands' jobs carried personal meaning connected with their relationship with their fathers or had compensated for the lack of that relationship. The reader may remember Mr Treacher whose father had 'rubbished' him and rarely allowed him to do anything for himself. Over the years his boss at work had not 'rubbished' him and he functioned adequately, although obsessively. A change of boss to a man who countermanded his decisions again left him feeling 'rubbished' and depressed enough to take himself to his GP. Mr Salmon's choice of job had been related to his father's aspirations and need to please him. When he left the police force (the picket lines in the 1984 miners' strike being too painful for him), his failure to establish his own business left him and his wife communicating only when they were quarrelling. Mrs Salmon's father had also enjoined on her that she was to better herself.

The plight of Mr and Mrs Holloway after he was made redundant vividly illustrates the continuing influence of a lost father after loss of job and the centrality of this theme in their marital problem. Both their fathers had deserted and both of them had learned to be self-sufficient. On his redundancy, Mr Holloway soon became quite immobilised, unable to look for another job. His grief for loss of job was doubled by loss of image of his father's love. The grief he had not allowed himself to experience many years previously when he, like Mrs Holloway, had become the responsible member of the family broke the defensive barriers. Mrs Holloway could not tolerate his passivity and his staying in bed all day, only going out to walk the dog. She had lost the safe, reliable man she had married and her newly found dependence had not yet developed into a more appropriate interdependence. This left her feeling more vulnerable than she had allowed herself to feel as a child. Fortunately her brittle independence did not reassert itself, but her daily tears and reproaches trebled Mr Holloway's misery. This behaviour confirmed his underlying fear that he, like his father, was only an untrustworthy and unreliable husband. Divided by their separate but mutual miseries about fathers, Mrs Holloway's tears and confusion increased enough for her to go to her GP. Her symptoms and her description of her fury with her husband got them referred for marital therapy which needed to centre on images of men and fathers.

Loss of job had great impact on some marriages when over the years the job had provided a channel of expression for feelings seemingly dangerous and needing to be sublimated. Sex had never been 'much at all' for Mrs Kettlewell. It had occurred only on his demand, but she never said 'No', because if she offended him in any way he retreated into a massive silence lasting for days or weeks and again took on extra work. But she valued the not 'much at all', because this was the one thing in which they were 'at least' together.

When Mr Kettlewell was discharged from the prison service he visibly lost confidence and within the fortnight became impotent. He regained his potency two years later when he acquired a job as a bailiff executing court writs. Work as a prison officer was to him, but eventually not to the prison service, an acceptable outlet for his sadism. Probably quite unconsciously both he and Mrs Kettlewell feared the degree of sadism that might have been expressed in the sexual act when there was no other outlet.

Mr and Mrs Pierce had a problem in respect of their confused feelings about expression of aggression and identity. Mr Pierce had wanted to be a hairdresser, but his parents would not hear of this and pushed him in the direction of 'manly pursuits'. He eventually ended up in management. His redundancy was called early retirement, as he was then aged 50. He felt very hurt by the way things had ended, his desk being moved before he had finished working on it. For a year he had not looked for another job, for the time being contented with reading and taking care of the house and their young son, aged two. For the time being they had enough money to live on in their accustomed life-style.

Mrs Pierce, an assertive woman after she realised that she was bigger than her bully of a father, complained to the counsellor that she was terrified of Mr Pierce's anger when he threw objects round the room. Although he never hit her, she feared he might do so. It soon became clear, however, that she was more terrified of his passivity in not looking for another job. She found herself thinking up ways to get him moving; why did he not start jogging? The more she urged him into another job, the more she goaded him into these outbursts. The combination of Mr Pierce's relief at being out of a job he never really wanted, although he had done it quite well, and his anger at the way he had been treated, and his wife's lack of ease at his taking on a role she had not been able to sustain herself, left them disturbed. In the counselling it became clear that Mrs Pierce had big doubts about herself as a woman and needed her husband to be in an overtly masculine role to contain her own assertive stance. Feeling desperately uncontained when he was the one at home caring for their son, she provoked him into the anger she had so feared as a child.

Multiple losses

It was not only early losses which made some of our clients so vulnerable to loss of job. Some of the most distressed or immobilised had been affected by multiple losses over recent years or concurrently. Mr Treacher's most bizarre behaviour occurred on the threat of double loss – loss of job and threat of loss of wife when 'nasties' inside her had been diagnosed.

The clergyman who worked with Mr and Mrs Latimer first met them when he conducted the funeral of Mr Latimer's father. Initially he saw his task as helping the family to mourn this loss. Soon it was clear that Mr and Mrs Latimer, in their late thirties, had a marital problem and had engineered a life-style which left them socially rejected and isolated. The vicar also learnt of Mr Latimer's unemployment (loss of job), of Mrs Latimer's recent hysterectomy (loss of body organ at a comparatively early age), and of Mr Latimer's mother's recent psychiatric breakdown which necessitated her admission to hospital. The 'thread of continuity' in their lives had been broken on four fronts.

When Mr Salmon left the police force, he and his wife chose to leave the north-east and set up business in 'sunny' Devon where they had once had an 'idyllic' holiday. When the new business failed, they really experienced the loss of the close-knit working-class community in which they had both grown up and which both their parents had wanted them to outgrow.

Mr Walton (who was so depressed and withdrawn following the threat of redundancy, afraid of his powerful mother saying, 'I told you so') and his wife had three children. The youngest, the only boy, aged four, was mentally handicapped. They had never faced up to their feelings about this, but when pressed to talk about them in the counselling, it emerged that Mrs Walton felt particularly guilty because she had 'talked' Mr Walton into having a third child. In addition, both her mother and her sister had cancer, the sister with secondary growths, the mother terminally ill. Three threats of major losses – of mother, of sister and of job – breached the defences they had erected against the anguish of having produced a damaged baby and the inherent loss of a fit and healthy son.

Sometimes a double loss was immediate and totally work-centred – a wife losing a job within months of her husband doing so. For several of our clients, the husband's redundancy coincided with a normal life-transition, quite often that of the children leaving home. Mrs Parker lost her part-time job shortly after Mr Parker had negotiated his redundancy, but she was also a recently 'redundant' mother as over the previous few years all four children had left home.

Mr and Mrs Rowlands' marital problem came to a head six years after Mr Rowlands became unemployed but at a time when they were alternately booting their 19-year-old son out of the house and Mrs Rowlands was manoeuvring him back again. As we stated in Chapter 4, we do not know whether they would have found it easier to let him grow up and leave home if Mr Rowlands had been in work and Mrs Rowlands had been more satisfied with her job. A trained nurse, she worked part-time on night duty at a small local hospital, but felt 'pushed past' by a lot of younger women with more up-to-date technical knowledge. She complained bitterly that her long years of experience now carried no weight. We can guess that with one partner unemployed, the other partner dissatisfied and feeling undervalued in her job, the redundancy of parenthood would weigh heavily, and particularly for this couple as up to the age of 13 the boy had been severely asthmatic and very clinging.

(In contrast to most of our families, Mrs Yoxall was in a state of agitation when she applied for marital counselling. Her husband, after years of irregular work and long spells of unemployment, had obtained a post with salary, perks and prospects better than he had ever achieved before. Her marriage was breaking up, she complained, and it was all her fault. On the four or five occasions when Mr Yoxall had been made redundant in the past they had always been upset, but they had never let it get them down for long. With her encouragement and support he had used his initiative in finding alternative work. She felt she ought to be pleased with the money, company car, and position they now had. She was not. Mr Yoxall was not at home as much as he used to be and she knew that the more she agitated, nagged and complained, the longer he spent at work. If he failed to telephone when held up, she imagined him, either with another woman or lying dead. It seemed that through the years of irregular work and bouts of unemployment her support of him gave her a role and sense of value. Now he was settled in a good job, she was the redundant one, and this happened for her at a time when the family was breaking up, the 18-year-old son job-hunting around the country and a 15 and 12-year-old increasingly out and about on their own and needing less of her attention.)

Our findings that loss of job severely affected people who had experienced severe deprivation in childhood or who were suffering from other concurrent losses or threat of loss are supported by studies of nightmares and combat neurosis. Lidz, writing in 1946, found in his studies of persistent and repetitive nightmares after combat and when physical safety had been assured, that many of the men had come from broken homes. He emphasised that this was the most important of the predisposing factors. 'The instability of the home was particularly severe among the sufferers. Absence of affection or insecurity of affection had left a lasting scar.'[1] When the nightmares occurred some considerable time after the traumatic event, they appeared subsequent to the loss of an emotionally significant person. The findings of Hartmann, writing on post-traumatic nightmares in 1984, substantiated those of Lidz: 'The nightmares may disappear for a time, and then suddenly may be reactivated by a later loss or rejection of some kind.'[2]

The moral

This book is not about the process of therapy, casework or counselling. Most professionals are well aware of the importance of helping people to engage in the process of mourning when there is some major loss to be mourned.

Many of the clients in our samples responded surprisingly quickly when the professionals related directly to their unemployed status and encouraged them to talk about their feelings, often having neglected to do this adequately before. However, our experience on this project led us to understand that with those who had been severely deprived either in the distant or recent past, giving attention just to the loss of work was not enough. When the grief from loss of work reverberated on an earlier loss, attention needed to be directed to the latter. For example, Mr and Mrs Walton made some progress in re-establishing their relationship, Mr Walton less withdrawn and Mrs Walton less anxiously attempting to control him, when the counsellor focussed on the problem of Mr Walton's promotion to a desk job and fear of his mother saying, 'I told you so'. However, the work then became very stuck and under any small stress their relationship deteriorated again. It was only when the counsellor paid more attention to the loss of a healthy male child and Mrs Walton shared her guilt about persuading her husband into their conceiving a third baby that they were able to sustain the improvement. Incidentally, the child's behaviour then became less hyperactive. Even so they could not re-establish their sexual relationship; presumably the image of the disastrous consequences of heterosexuality still affected their previously normal sexual drive.

Mr Holloway was able to get away from the television and search for another job when, in the safety of the therapy, he had allowed himself to grieve for the loss of his father in his early teens and understood how much the job had carried for him as a symbol of his father's love. As his anger about his father came more to the fore and met that of his wife about her deserting father, the symptoms which took her to the GP were relieved, but their marriage became more acrimonious. Tears, confusion and resentful reproach gave way to rows, the old suppressed feelings now on the surface, but in the absence of the actual fathers, directed at the nearest butt – each other.

Then, as they acquired more understanding of what was happening and of the unreal expectations they both placed on Mr Holloway to be the all-providing father neither of them had had, they were able to relinquish the illusion of being able to put clocks back and relate more to the reality of each other's strengths and weaknesses and to each other's losses and sorrows. Only then did the rows abate and were they able to take stock of their situation and consider alternatives of Mr Holloway's re-training or starting a small business, and moving house to enable them to do this. Finally Mr Holloway obtained another job, not as good as the one he had lost, but they were confident enough of each other to start trying for the baby which they both wanted but which they had not dared to do before.

7

Daylight Robbery

Damn them! They will not let my play run, but they steal my
thunder.

W.S. Walsh

It is certain that envy is the worst sin that is; for all other sins
are sins only against one virtue, whereas envy is against all
virtue and against all goodness.

Chaucer

In Chapter 3 we wrote of the use which couples made of 'the
morning that separates'. Employment of one or both partners
allowed them a structured distance and independence from
each other. When this structure ceases to be available, a major
adaptation in the marriage is required, either to a reduced
distance or to the creation of other means of achieving
distance. Much has been written about this in relation to
retirement,[1] which is thought by many to be one of the most
fraught transitional crises in life. And this is considered to be
so despite the fact that there have usually been several years of
anticipation and often a physical and mental slowing down – a
readiness to take life more easily than previously.

In circumstances of enforced premature retirement from
work in youth or early middle age, the problem of managing
increased or constant togetherness can be immense for many
married partners, particularly if they are experiencing
difficulty in handling their joint grief for all the incurred losses.
As Mr Bell said, 'We see each other 24 hours a day.'

It is not, however, just the problem of the previously working
spouse in having to adjust to becoming home-based throughout
the day, finding ways of filling his time, and without means of
escape from his partner. Previously non-working partners,
used to having the house to themselves for the major part of

the day, can be just as much affected when they lose their freedom in the use of what had been *their* space from 8 a.m. to 6 p.m. for much of the week. 'Oh, I would love him to go off and get out from under my feet sometimes' is the *cri de coeur* of many a housewife after her husband's retirement or redundancy.

The problem of too much togetherness is obviously increased in small, inadequate or impoverished housing – not enough room to escape – and with reduced finances which curtail separate outings and leisure pursuits – not enough financial leeway with which to achieve the much needed distance. When Mr Marks became unemployed he could not afford the one hobby which he enjoyed and which he was good at: snooker. A game at the club gave him the opportunity to meet his old work mates, but a session cost £5.

In addition, when one working partner has made his main contribution to the maintenance of the home through his external labour and earnings, there will on his redundancy need to be a re-assignment of roles within the domestic sphere. Usually one or both partners will expect a redistribution of domestic tasks, although each may have different ideas as to what this will be.

This chapter is about the problems experienced by couples in our samples in handling the situation of too much togetherness, their difficulties in re-assigning domestic roles and their failure in making adequate or appropriate adjustment to their new circumstances which left them so uncomfortable or unsatisfied in their relationship. They asked for help or came to the attention of the professional helpers either through the 'illness model', delinquency, baby care or some other model whereby they signalled their distress, as we described in Chapter 4. They were unlike Harry and Vera Boyle in Douglas Dunn's short story, 'Getting Used to It':[2]

Several days a week, after lunch, Harry and Vera Boyle spent an hour in bed. To begin with, it seemed an extraordinary thing to do, as if, were they discovered, it might bring unemployment into disrepute.

'I suppose,' Vera said, 'that this is what rich people do in the afternoon. I could get used to it.'

'I'm getting used to it already.' Harry did more housework than he had been brought up to believe was good for a man's dignity. 'How much would it cost,' he asked Vera, 'to have those curtains dry cleaned?'

'I don't like what's happening to you. Last week you washed the kitchen floor, behind my back. And now you're talking about curtains.'

A few days later: 'Have we any carpet shampoo in the house, Vera? I don't see it in the cupboard.'

'Have you spilled something?'

'No, but look at it. It's a good few shades darker than when we bought it.'

Carpet shampoo materialised, as Vera took advantage of Harry's new housewifery, or husbandry.

'I think it's getting to you,' said Vera.

'What is?'

'Unemployment is. And time is too.'

'You don't hear me talk about unemployment. I just don't get roused by the subject. I've got plenty of time.'

'You were certainly angry enough the night you came home with that redundancy notice.'

'Sure, I was livid. But right now I'm into carpets and curtains. I'm a home boy. If they can keep me on the breadline, plus some, I'll be happy enough and so will you.'

'Guess who's your "plus some"?'

'What?'

'Me.' Vera smiled.

'Too close – too far'

In contrast to Harry and Vera, for many of our couples less actual distance increased their anxiety about intimacy; their partner ceased to be a 'plus some'. In pushing up barriers against too much emotional or domestic intrusion, they sometimes drove each other further apart than when provided with a structured means of escape from each other. Byng-Hall has called this the 'too close – too far' system, whereby couples get themselves into a position in which the space they create to free themselves from the anxiety concerning too much closeness or intimacy becomes 'so distant as to make them feel constantly insecure'.[3]

After a period of excessive house renovation, Mr Morrison, previously described as a 'good husband', started to 'escape' out of the house for longer periods than he would have been absent while in paid employment. He claimed that he was doing 'odd jobs' for other people, but his wife heard no details of these jobs, nor saw the supposed private earnings. Getting no help from her husband and with the additional babies, she became increasingly resentful' and perpetually nagging when he was there to be nagged at. Mr Morrison stayed out even longer hours and a vicious circle was set up.

Mr Morrison may also have been escaping from the eldest child who had become demanding and endlessly attention-seeking, temper tantrums succeeding each other with endless monotony. Which was the chicken and which was the egg? Was the child reacting to the marital discord, or the father escaping from the whining toddler? – another vicious circle.

Mr Ryan was explicit that his escape was from a crying baby. He himself had been a deprived child; in the absence of a neglectful mother, he had been 'dragged up' by his older sisters. He could not bear the needs of his own baby not being met immediately by his wife. (We may guess that he was kept waiting too long by his sisters.) Neighbours became concerned about his rough handling of the baby whom the health visitor then had admitted to hospital on 'social grounds – feeding difficulties due to tension in the home'. When the social worker was called in, Mr Ryan was quite clear that it was 'too dangerous' for the baby to be left with him when Mrs Ryan was out doing a few hours a week part-time work. It seemed that the cries of this young baby reactivated the primitive rage that he had been left with in the circumstances of his own neglected infancy.

The social worker suggested that Mr Ryan spent more time on his allotment, but Mrs Ryan could not tolerate this idea. Although she had previously been able to allow him to go to work, her basic insecurity (she had also suffered extreme deprivation – 'adopted, rejected by adoptive parents; fostered, rejected by foster parents') was heightened by her husband's redundancy. She experienced his going to the allotment as desertion and insisted on his staying with her 'to listen for the baby' (the real crying baby and, we suggest, the crying infant inside her adult self).

Mr and Mrs Ryan's second baby, as several others in our samples, was conceived immediately or soon after the threat of redundancy, or actual redundancy. Whereas some of the husbands lost their potency, others became more sexually active than they had been when in work. Mr Norton was often impotent when working, but he and his wife maintained that this had not worried them. They worked together, their marriage seemingly based on a work contract with each other, but with some doubt intruding as to whether they had contracted a relationship in which to bring up children. When they were threatened with the possibility of no work, their current job about to come to an end, Mr Norton announced one evening after a party, 'I'm going to get you pregnant.' Mrs Norton replied, 'I dare you.' And he did.

For some couples, the desire for closeness expressed through increased sexual intimacy was, no doubt, a natural reaction whereby they sought reassurance against fears concerning survival when a regular pay packet ceased, and, in Klein's terms, against the linked threat of loss of love. Some of the wives complained of feeling 'used', and of receiving little regard for their needs or tiredness. The compulsion behind the increased sexual drive of some husbands indicated desperate attempts to compensate; when they were deprived of one means of expressing their potency through exercise of skill and earning capacity, it seemed they needed to overstate another aspect of their masculinity.

However, the degree of increased or excessive intimacy *in bed* frightened some couples and in Byng-Hall's terms they pushed each other away *out of bed*. Mrs Todd went on her own to a marriage guidance counsellor. She complained of her husband's spitefulness about her new pregnancy and his insistence on an abortion. When she talked in more detail about their circumstances, his recent redundancy, the financial problem of a third child, and yet her distaste for an abortion, she also talked of his (to her) recent sexual excesses. Excessive sex, it seemed, had reduced physical distance but, combined with spite, had increased emotional distance.

Shadows

When a job had been held as an important symbol of masculinity, the loss of that job and continued unemployment had a greater impact on the loser and the spouse than was usually so with couples who held less rigid images of respective roles and had previously shared some domestic and child care tasks. Yet Mr Morrison had taken an active role as father when he was in work. When out of work and after his excessive and ill-timed maintenance of the house, he did less and less, not only driven away by the reproaches of his wife and the cries of the eldest child, but also as if, when not in work, he seemed threatened by the prospect of becoming 'all woman'.

Mr Ryan told the social worker how he had 'blown his top' one evening when he came downstairs and found that Mrs Ryan had *laid the fire*. This activity – normally his job – had been in his eyes the only remaining vestige of his masculinity.

Mr Skelton became long-term unemployed after an accident which prevented his doing the heavy, outdoor building work he had done for years and which required considerable strength. Loss of a *heavy* job dealt a severe blow to his self-esteem. Keeping strong and fit had been a particular factor in his upbringing. In adulthood he dismissed light work as 'woman's work'. He and his wife maintained traditional, highly differentiated roles. Mrs Skelton cared for the house and their four children; the home was her territory. Mr Skelton's world revolved round heavy work, the garden and the pub.

On his unemployment, Mrs Skelton complained about his getting in her way, 'always there', sitting in a chair in the corner; she did not want him interfering. Increasingly she banished him from her territory into the garden. When he sought refuge from wind and rain, using the housekeeping money to purchase beer at the pub, the rows between them became more frequent. Eventually she expelled him completely from the house and set him up in a nearby flat. He was allowed back home only to dig the garden. 'Robbed' of his sense of identity and masculinity, and his home, he became, needless to say, a shadow of his former self.

It takes two people to create a situation like this – one who reduces to a shadow and another who becomes such a shadow. Mr Skelton's collapse is understandable in terms of his history and internal image of masculinity. In terms of his body-image he had much to grieve. We do not know in what circumstances Mrs Skelton grew up in that she so encouraged his collapse. Presumably something in her was severely threatened once he ceased to fulfil her image that men must be strong. In her newly aroused anxiety that she could not depend on him in the way she had been used to do, unable to tolerate his disability and his and her grief concerning their losses, including his strength, she further reduced his sense of potency. We may guess that both their sets of parents had lived highly differentiated roles and that neither of them knew from past experience how to adapt, nor how to create some form of sharing together.

Mr Skelton was not, in fact, incapable in the house. For a period of a few days before he was finally banished, Mrs Skelton was largely immobilised, having hurt her back. Greeting the social worker in her dressing gown, she attributed this state to her having fallen downstairs. (One of the children told the social worker that his father had 'thrown' her when he came home 'the worse for drink'.) However, in these circumstances Mr Skelton was like a 'happy, busy mother', making tea for the adults and frying chips for the children's meal. It seemed that he was only allowed, or able to take, a role when she was incapacitated and he could be fully in control.

In the social worker's discussions with them about the youngest son's delinquency (the reason for her contact with them), Mrs Skelton always over-rode any suggestion Mr Skelton made on behalf of the boy. When she was physically in control again, she re-assumed parental control. And finally Mr Skelton agreed with her that there was no place for him in the home.

Mr and Mrs Skelton were one of several couples in our samples who, unlike Harry and Vera Boyle, did not know how to share, and the unemployed husbands became shadows in the wake of their wives. Some of Mr Todd's spite, and Mr Skelton's drinking and 'throwing' Mrs Skelton down the stairs, may have been reactive to their wives' control and gross over-activity. Mr Todd's unemployment re-invoked in Mrs Todd an image established in childhood that men are competent only in impregnating women who are then left to do all the work. Her basic, underlying insecurity heightened when Mr Todd lost his job. Newly pregnant, she cleaned the house harder than ever, organised children and home, and took part-time seasonal jobs to ease the financial situation. The more she did, the more redundant, and the more sexually excessive and spiteful Mr Todd became.

When Mr Parker was employed, he took all the decisions without consulting his wife. This seemed to be a reaction to his having experienced his mother as having made all the decisions when he was a child. It was as if he feared that if he let his wife share in the decision making, she would take over completely. On his unemployment, she did just that. Two years after his redundancy, the previously dignified, professional man had become 'sheepish, defeated, and folded into his chair'. 'My dignity is being eroded,' he said. Face to face most of every day, she now asserted 20 years of pent-up resentment. He liked to cook, but he got under her feet in the kitchen; 'Yes, he cooked a good meal, but he used too many pans.' He was so slow in the house; she had the dishes washed, the house vacuumed and the washing on the line, and he still had not finished the job he was on. Like Mr Streatfield, described in Chapter 4, he was complained against for not helping, but, when he did, he was charged with 'You're not doing it properly.'

From under one's eyes

Mr Parker, Mr Skelton and Mr Todd all felt robbed of their manhood and became shadows of their former selves. Robbery was one of the most vivid images with which our sample presented us. We were interested in the number of times the word *stolen* was used, as it was by the miners in the long strike of 1984/85. Yet it was not just the husbands who felt robbed. Even more vivid and numerous were the families in which the husbands, feeling robbed of a job, then robbed their wives of theirs.

When the vicar first called on Mr and Mrs Latimer after the death of Mr Latimer's mother and learned of all their losses, including Mr Latimer's job, the household generally seemed to be a hive of activity. In contrast, Mrs Latimer sat silently in the corner of the room. Mr Latimer did all the talking and described the domestic chores he was doing, the shopping, the taking of the children to school and his management of the benefit payments. He was obviously industrious and seemingly ingenious. The house was well furnished; furniture, bought at junk shops, was restored to a high standard. The vicar felt on this and subsequent visits that he was constantly being asked to confirm how well Mr Latimer was managing in their current difficult circumstances.

Three months later Mr Latimer obtained a job. Seen on her

own, the previously silent Mrs Latimer came to life. She was friendly, talkative and lively, and it soon emerged that she was the furniture restorer. It seemed that now Mr Latimer was again working, she could repossess her own life and hobby.

Mrs Murray was not able to repossess her life two years after her husband's redundancy. A previously placid and friendly woman had lost weight and was 'edgy and fidgety' with big hollows under her eyes. 'I have no life of my own,' she said, as she burst into tears. Mr Murray was 'always there' and organised everything in the house. He insisted on helping, but actually supervised. If she ordered three pints of milk, he would change the order to one. If they went shopping together, as he insisted they did, she would find when they reached the cash-desk that he had removed several of the products she had chosen and substituted others for them.

She encouraged him to pursue his own interests, but he said it was better for him to help her so they could spend the afternoon together; but when it came to afternoons, he drank three pints of beer and then slept. She had taken a small part-time job 'to keep herself sane'. On the surface he expressed pleasure about this, but she felt he resented it. On the days she was at home, he continued to 'help' her; on the days she was out, he did nothing and she returned to the washing up, no shopping, no prepared meal and the house in a mess. Sadly, she said she wished she were young enough to have another baby. At least he could not *steal* that from her.

Mrs Street did have another baby, as did several of the wives in our sample. She then enquired of the health visitor on behalf of her husband about hormone treatment. He had read about 'a guy in America who had this, so that he could feed the baby'.

How can this sort of behaviour be explained?

We believe that Mr Murray's and Mr Street's behaviour was an expression of extreme envy, characterised, as it so often is, by a devaluation of the envied person. Envy has been described as 'a base passion drawing the worst passions in its train',[4] but it is always important when trying to understand the depth of envy to distinguish it from jealousy (the two words often used synonymously in everyday parlance). In this book, we use Melanie Klein's definitions:[5]

Envy is the angry feeling that another possesses and enjoys

something desirable – *the envious impulse being to take it away or to spoil it* [our italics].

Moreover, envy implies the subject's relation to one person only and goes back to the earliest, exclusive relation with the mother.

Jealousy is based on envy, but involves a relation to at least two people; it is mainly concerned with love that the subject feels is his due and has been taken away, or is in danger of being taken away, from him by his rival. In the everyday conception of jealousy, a man or woman feels deprived of the loved person by somebody else.

It is difficult to imagine that any person exists who does not at times, or even frequently, feel envy. Life is notoriously unfair and we are surrounded by others whose abilities and possessions outstrip our own. The employed are obviously a potent source of envy to the unemployed who wish to work. There can be little dispute about this. (Perhaps there is more dispute about the over-employed person's envy of the unemployed. As Harry and Vera wondered, does unemployment fall into disrepute if the unemployed enjoy themselves in bed in the afternoon? Does the 'Get on your bike' brigade protest too much about the laziness of the unemployed when after too many over-long working days, their wives complain so bitterly?) The emotion is universal, but the strength of it and the ability to handle it varies enormously from one person to another. Apparently Harry and Vera could handle it. At first, Vera was disturbed when Harry started to take on a new role in the house. Yet she was able to allow him to get into curtains and carpets, because he never set about destroying her. They handled their initial discomfort in their re-assignment of roles through their mutual pleasure in and gratitude towards each other.

Gratitude is one of the main derivatives of love; envy is one of the strongest antidotes to love and gratitude. Many of the couples in our samples were unable to mobilise their gratitude to each other in their newly deprived circumstances and, with their envy roused, they displayed immense difficulty in handling it. We believe that this problem, like their problem of mourning their losses, dated back to their early deprivation, some of which we described in Chapter 6.

Envy has its roots in the innate and primitive anxiety of early infancy when food and care are withheld. When need becomes ravenous, it feels insatiable. Increasingly the mother is seen as the possessor of that much needed food and love. If she, or her substitute, withhold what is needed beyond the limited toleration of the infant, the innate primitive rage seeks only to destroy that source. According to Klein, every baby gets consumed with this primitive rage but (to use Winnicott's term) the 'good enough' mother, the source of nourishment and care and, therefore, of life itself, returns. Time and time again the baby learns that his hatred did not destroy. Repeated experiences of regained enjoyment and then of gratitude slowly mitigate the destructive impulse. In this way, the mother imparts more than nourishment; she lays the foundation of future ability to trust and hope, to enjoy and to be grateful for that enjoyment.

Envy is never entirely mitigated and its impulse to take or to destroy what is needed for the self continues to be expressed in childhood by repeated claims for time and attention beyond actual need. It is often expressed symbolically by theft, usually in the home and from the mother, not with delinquent, anti-social intent, but as if a *taking by right*. Most young children steal in this way, often in front of the mother's eyes, but normally the basic impulse continues to be mitigated or repressed by a developing moral conscience. When stealing persists, extends beyond the home and has a compulsive, senseless quality, it can still be understood as a symbolic claiming of a right, a deep underlying conflict and a signal for help. What is perceived as greed in the older child or adult is often the continued expression of what initially was need. Only when secondary gains become an end in themselves does stealing take on the character of a conscious, thought-out, criminal act.

If jobs are felt by some people to be a 'right' – not a moral right, but a right in terms of a basic need for survival, physical and emotional nourishment, it is not surprising that, when jobs are lost, the word *stolen* is used so often and so much unconscious, compulsive robbery takes place.

We do not believe that Mr Murray was aware of his envy of Mrs Murray, nor that she would have explained his behaviour in these terms. All she knew was that she felt destroyed and stolen from and dearly wished she could do one thing which he could not take from her – bear another baby. We suspect that Mr Murray's underlying envy and anger had been well repressed throughout much of his life (unlike that of Harry and Vera which had been mitigated). Apparently it had not been a factor in their marriage before his redundancy, nor, as far as we know, interfered with his work performance or relationships with his colleagues. In fact, sublimated in his work, it may have been the spur behind his success. Without this outlet, his defences failed, or we may say, he was robbed of a means of defence.

Or we can understand his behaviour in a more positive light. He was a well educated man and his reason told him that he had no right to be so angry about new technologies, whereby he had lost his job. When he could not find words, or reason, to explain the depth of his feeling or why he felt so bad, he tried to get closer to Mrs Murray and show her what it felt like to be him, by doing to her what he felt had been done to him. This type of manoeuvre is a very common phenomenon when feelings have been severely repressed and out of conscious reach; actions over which the subject has little control are used instead of words as the impulse fights for expression.

This phenomenon can occur in conjunction with, and be reinforced by, other external circumstances and internal images. Mrs Latimer appeared to suffer less than Mrs Murray. We do not know whether she would have been in a similar state if Mr Latimer's unemployment had been more protracted. Yet she let Mr Latimer steal her role, even to the extent of his claiming her hobby and skill as his own, as if she had some sympathy with him. However, she went along with his take-over bid at a time when she was recovering from a major operation. And, like many of our other couples, neither she nor Mr Latimer had had much experience of their parents' sharing. She had been brought up by her father after her mother's desertion, but claimed that her life as a child had continued to be so awful that anything was better than that. Now she was learning that a man could look after her and the children well. Mr Latimer's father had held his family together during his mother's long-term psychiatric illness. Both of them had more faith in men's, rather than women's, ability to care.

There were other wives who gave up their productivity when their husbands were deprived of theirs. A pint-sized Mrs Marks arrived at the vicar's house one evening, 'because of family problems'. Mr Marks, formerly a shipyard worker, had been unemployed four years and had become another shadow. Then the Job Centre offered him six weeks' work abroad. He took this job, worked long hours, sent big money home and wrote regularly of his pleasure in 'being useful again'. Mrs Marks seemed to grow in size and said she now felt a 'proper married woman'. In forging a link with her husband, she threw herself into voluntary work in the parish. When Mr Marks' contract ended, they were thrilled to be together again. The former shadow accompanied his wife to church and turned out to be a tall, well-built and striking man. They had the honeymoon which previously they had not been able to afford.

Unemployed again, the feelings of loss and despair took over once more and, after the respite and renewal of hope, were worse than previously. 'Volcanoes' of rows were triggered by Mr Marks' resentment (envy) that Mrs Marks had now found some fulfilment in her voluntary work. She enjoyed it and it cost them nothing, whereas his snooker cost £5 a session.

Soon Mrs Marks started to˙ withdraw from her parish activities. As she said, she felt 'obliged to stop'. If he were disabled, she could not let herself be able. Curtains were literally drawn and the front door bell left unanswered. When the vicar finally obtained entry again, Mrs Marks had succumbed to a series of chest infections which prevented her leaving the house. Mr Marks was just morose and unwilling to talk. The persistence of the vicar and his lay helpers finally enabled curtains to be drawn back. Mrs Marks resumed some of her activities and Mr Marks was accompanying her to church, but in company remained totally silent.

We suggest that when the wives protected their husbands to this extent they too had a problem about unmitigated envy, unable to tolerate its expression or to withstand it. When their husbands were expressing the envy so dramatically, they did not need to know about their own. Extreme lack of confidence in themselves must have contributed to their handing over the role. The stealers seemed to do the housekeeping so much more efficiently than they could do themselves. Extreme envy, if not counteracted by attempts to take over and destroy, leaves the subject feeling completely empty, and all the feelings of goodness and strength get projected into the envied. In the mutual projective system, which we described in Chapter 3, one partner carried all the drive for them both, the other the emptiness for them both. And this was so, but the other way round for the couples in which the busy, bossy wives contributed to their husband's increasing shadowyness; too insecure to experience help as help, perceiving it only as a threat to their own often phoney competence, they carried all the drive and power and the husbands carried all the emptiness.

Mrs Roker was one of the wives who left herself empty, feeling that her husband did it better than she, particularly in respect of his managing the benefit 'without getting into debt', with the implication that she would have done so. In her words, he was doing an excellent job, everything in the house spotless and in its place – real army style.

It was Sheila, their seven-year-old daughter, who sent up the signal for help. The health visitor received a call from the school. Sheila was causing concern because she was *stealing* – 'only petty things', but the teacher was amazed that she took these things 'right in front of my eyes', and then denied that she had done so. Mr and Mrs Roker knew about this, but as far as they were concerned Sheila was getting on well, there was nothing to worry about except that the school should be more vigilant; it was the teacher's job to prevent the thefts.

At a meeting at the school, which Mr and Mrs Roker and the health visitor attended, Mr and Mrs Roker still maintained there was nothing to worry about. When the teacher asked who brought Sheila to school, Mrs Roker replied that she did. Mr Roker looked surprised and asked her if she was sure about this. The health visitor then realised, although she had never queried it before, that it was always Mr Roker who brought the younger children to the clinic, and on her home visits he was the one who spoke of the children's progress. She encouraged Mr and Mrs Roker to talk about themselves. The meeting learned that Mr Roker had been in the army, but at the end of his contract had no civilian skill. Initially he had spent his time putting their new home and garden in order. Mrs Roker had cared for the children and had had another baby.

At about this time, Mr Roker had stopped looking for work

because he 'now had a job', washing, ironing, cooking, cleaning, shopping and caring for the children. When Mrs Roker was asked what she felt about this, she burst into tears and said she 'didn't have a place now', but Mr Roker was doing an excellent job. She left the house about 5.30 each evening and either went to the house of a woman friend or wandered the streets, returning home after midnight.

Immediately after this meeting, when Mr Roker's theft came out into the open, Sheila's stealing from under the teacher's eyes ceased. Mr and Mrs Roker started talking to each other more than they had ever done before in their married life, but, as Mrs Roker explained to the health visitor, the problem, as she saw it, was that Mr Roker enjoyed his job as houseperson and did not want to give it up.

A few weeks later, she looked brighter and happier and announced that she was pregnant again. When this turned out to be a false alarm, she was depressed and complained that Mr Roker was ill-treating Sheila, constantly picking on her and doing nothing for her. This was contrary to what the health visitor had observed over previous months, remembering numerous occasions when Sheila had turned for comfort to her father rather than to her mother. Another few weeks later, Mrs Roker was properly pregnant and, having regained a role for herself, was buoyantly happy.

For health visitors and social workers, however, this type of situation remains worrying. There were several other wives in our samples who, with their roles stolen, had taken to wandering the streets, not, we thought, with initial intent to prostitute themselves. But what, apart from their basic unhappiness and emptiness, would this lead to? Did they, like Mrs Roker, have to go on having babies to maintain a role, or to become the earner through prostitution to support all those extra babies? We suspect the pregnancy was so important, not just because it was a role the husband could not steal, but also because the live baby in the womb helped to counteract the feeling of emptiness. (Mrs Yates, not in either of our samples, told one of us in her therapy that she had had her five children, although she had no time or real concern for them, not because the pregnancies made her feel so good, but because *half an hour* of those pregnancies made her feel a whole, real person. She spent the rest of the pregnancies feeling sick, but it was worth it for those five half-hours.)

When wives are ousted to the extent of wandering the streets in their unemployed state – and on our Devon workshop we had visions of crocodiles of women wandering round Ashburton, Bovey Tracey, Bideford and Barnstaple – the oldest girl child immediately becomes at risk of incest. Had Mr Roker, we wondered, started treating Sheila badly as a defence against her seeking comfort from him which was too sexually tantalising?

This case indicates the power of a family system which is presented so convincingly to the outside world. Until Sheila sent up the signal for help, the health visitor had been impressed how well the family, with the father unemployed, was managing. After the meeting at the school, she was concerned about what she had missed; Mr Roker had come to the clinic month after month and had discussed the children's developmental steps with such authority and military precision, that she had never questioned the absence of Mrs Roker. Like the child's stealing, it had all been 'right under my eyes'.

*

In the final part of this book, we look more closely at the problems encountered by workers who are employed to help the unemployed: the systems into which they are drawn, despite the signals for help; and the defences which they are invited to uphold.

PART III

EMPLOYED
TO HELP THE
UNEMPLOYED

He hated all good workers and vertuous deeds.

Spenser

8

Under the Influence

They have stolen his wits away.

De La Mare

The focus of this part of the book is on the interaction between employed and unemployed people. In this chapter we describe the relationship between unemployed client and employed practitioner. In Chapter 9 we look at the wider social and political context in which this professional relationship takes place.

In turning our attention to the practitioners in a variety of settings – our own, and other clinics, social services, probation, health visiting, marriage guidance and pastoral care, we are not writing about techniques; rather we are describing the experiences and feelings that were sometimes aroused in us and in the practitioners who joined us on the workshops in London, Devon and Tyneside when we were drawn into the emotional system of a family. The health visitor working with the Roker family was abashed when she realised what had been going on right under her eyes and that, in the face of Mr Roker's convincing discussions about the children, she had not queried Mrs Roker's absence. It is easy to say that this should not have happened, but such a statement does not advance our understanding of why such oversights continue to occur even when the practitioners are well-trained and experienced.

We write in the belief that by the very nature of humanity practitioners cannot expect to influence their clients if they do not take into account that the clients are also influencing them, both consciously and unconsciously; and that they work with a serious disadvantage if they fail to recognise this. We believe that practitioners who assume they are not affected or try not to be affected by their clients, ostensibly remaining unin-volved, are just as affected, but less knowingly and less usefully so than those who take account of their emotional involvement and spontaneous reactions, particularly when they find these reactions are out of character for them.

The lamentable therapist

One of the uses of working in this way is increased understanding of the client. If he has this effect on me, the practitioner who sees him once a week, he probably has a similar effect multiplied tenfold on his nearest relatives with whom he is in close association most of the time. As a way of working, it is based on the idea that when a problem is partly, largely or completely unconscious, it cannot be put into words. When things cannot be defined, other means of communication have to be found. One of the means clients can use in their attempts to get the practitioner to understand more about their plight is to get him to feel as they do, or to feel the feelings that are too frightening for them and from which they are defending themselves. This is usually done quite unconsciously.

Although we do not fully understand the actual mechanism,* we are aware from so many instances in our own practice and that of others that, as Freud said in 1915:

> It is a very remarkable thing that the unconscious of one human being can react upon that of another without passing through the conscious. ... descriptively speaking, the fact is incontestable.[1]

Many readers will be aware of this phenomenon when in particular empathy with another they find that they are imbued with feeling beyond their imaginative or identificatory efforts. They may also remember instances when captive to a friend pouring out his troubles, they are thanked profusely for

* 'Fifty years ago naturalists were content with the observation that bats catch moths. Then came the discovery that bats produce sounds inaudible to the human ear and use echoes to locate their prey. Now it appears that not only do moths have soundproofing, but that they have ears specifically designed to listen in to an approaching enemy transmitter. To counter this advance, bats developed an irregular flight path, which confused the moths until they in their turn came up with an ultrasonic jamming device. But bats still catch moths, and it can only be a matter of time before research discovers the next development in this escalating drama' (L. Watson, *Supernature*, London 1973).

their listening ear because the troubled person now feels so much better. Yet apparently it has not been just a sharing that has helped, as the captive listener finds that he now feels as uneasy and as anxious as the previously troubled friend who now departs more cheerfully. We are again talking of the mechanism of projection.

In professional practice we try to use these projections – the feelings we have had evoked in us during a session or are left with at the end – to increase our understanding, particularly when we know these feelings to be foreign to our general feeling state at the beginning of the session. (Obviously, if the practitioner is generally out of sorts that day – got out of bed like a bear with a sore head – this is his problem and not related to the client whom he sees at three o'clock in the afternoon.)

An example of this type of communication from a client – an important message which could not be put into words – was experienced by one of the project team over several sessions with one of his clients. We give this illustration from our own clinical practice in some detail to illustrate how we attempt to think about and use the interaction between the practitioner and his client to further our understanding of the client's psychological struggles.

The therapist felt that he was losing his memory when Mrs Acton, a seemingly competent and well organised person, started talking about various events in her life as if he had prior knowledge of them. Much practised at remembering the details of sessions and of his clients' life stories, he became increasingly confused, even disorientated, wondering why he had forgotten what she must previously have told him, and finally doubting his own competence – even his own sanity. Sharing this problem with his supervisor, he was reminded that he normally had a good memory. The supervisor queried what Mrs Acton was trying to tell him through her behaviour and the response she was eliciting from him. At the next session with Mrs Acton he was able to ask her if recently when her husband was suddenly made redundant, or earlier in her life, she had felt lost, left behind, utterly confused or frighteningly disorientated. Mrs Acton's managing, competent self started to deny that she ever felt confused; her husband (like the practitioner) was the confused one who was always forgetting; it drove her mad. And then she halted and burst into tears.

'Why are you crying?' he asked.

Slowly she explained that her parents had always seemed to be presenting her with *faits accomplis*. A new school, holiday arrangements and other big changes were thrust on her without warning. The most frightening disruption occurred when as a small child she and her mother had suddenly and without warning, as it seemed to her, left the house where they had been living since her birth and joined her father in another country. He was a complete stranger to her because his unemployment in the 1930s had occasioned his going abroad to find work and establish a home for them. Bringing the session back into the present, the therapist, no longer the disorientated one now that Mrs Acton was starting to get in touch with her own feelings, connected this experience of her childhood – her world constantly being turned upside down, leaving her quite lost and disorientated – with the recent experience of her and her husband's world being turned upside down when he was given his redundancy notice without warning. The therapist's ability to reflect on his feelings of disorientation in himself enabled him to relate to her feelings, to help her to hold them and to make them less frightening in the present than they were in the past because of the explanation of their origins. His feelings of losing his sanity had not resulted in actual madness, as hers need not. Temporary disorientation at a time of shock was normal, not mad.

His use of his own feeling gave him diagnostic help in a better understanding of Mrs Acton. It also helped him to understand the interaction between Mr and Mrs Acton. Mrs Acton had said that it was Mr Acton who was the confused one. When Mr Acton was feeling disorientated by his sudden redundancy and carrying his wife's projected feelings as well, he was carrying a double dose of feelings as we explained in Chapter 3. This double dose exaggerated his disorientated behaviour, thus increasing her fears about the danger of such feeling; it drove her mad, she said. The more she feared, the more she projected, the more he carried for the two of them, the more witless his behaviour became, and the more she feared and the more she projected, and the more this vicious spiral continued.

When Mrs Acton started to recognise her own feelings and ceased to project them into her husband, he became less disorientated and his behaviour less disturbing to her. She was then better able to tolerate both her and her husband's feeling of being 'thrown for six', as she now called it when they were assailed again by what had happened to them. Being 'thrown' was uncomfortable and distressing, particularly when they both felt 'thrown' at the same time, but it was not proving disastrous.

By studying his own experience with Mrs Acton and then using it in his work with her, the therapist was able to change his stance. His experience of feeling incompetent enabled him to ask a pertinent question and enabled Mrs Acton to confront her own anxiety. We believe the therapist's change of behaviour is of therapeutic value in its own right. It offers the client confidence that behaviour can change and it gives him more hope for himself than if he sees the therapist as 'the expert', a mentor from above, in full control and who never makes mistakes (with the implication that mistakes are not recoverable). Slowly Mrs Acton and the therapist found their way together towards an important understanding about her behaviour which radically changed their interaction and subsequently that of Mr and Mrs Acton.

This understanding was achieved through the therapist's use of what in technical language we call the countertransference – thoughts and feelings evoked in the practitioner by the client. The practitioner's countertransference is his response to the client's transference.

The client brings into the counselling relationship feelings, attitudes and defences which stem from an unconscious repetition of early formative relationships which are inappropriate in the present.[2] What is transferred is not a true representation of what actually happened in the past, but rather a configuration of the projections and introjections which were employed to make sense of and manage those early relationships with significant figures.

Joseph writes:

> By definition our use of the transference must include everything that the patient brings into the relationship. What he brings in can best be gauged by our focussing our attention

on what is going on within the relationship, how he is using the analyst, alongside and beyond what he is saying. Much of our understanding of the transference comes through our understanding of how patients act on us to feel things for varied reasons; how they unconsciously act out with us in the transference, trying to get us to act out with them; how they convey aspects of their inner world built up from infancy ... experiences often beyond the use of words, which we can often capture through the feelings aroused in us, through our countertransference ...[3]

A transference serves the patient in two ways. First, it allows unmanageable feelings to be got rid of. Secondly, it is a way of attempting to get in touch with another person by getting him to feel what it was like for the patient. As Jung has said, it is a form of bridge building.[4] Mrs Acton got rid of unmanageable feelings of disorientation and formed a sort of bridge with her therapist. She had experienced her mother as a remote person who did not explain what was going to happen. In a desperate attempt to deal with her confusion and to get closer to her mother, she tried to behave in the same remote way. When she portrayed this identification in her relationship with the therapist, she succeeded in getting him to feel as she had felt time and time again as a child, and then again when recently faced with the *fait accompli* of her husband's redundancy notice. 'It came out of the blue', she repeated over and over again. In anyone's terms, it was a frightening disruption of what had seemed a relatively predictable life-style. In Mrs Acton's internal world it reactivated the *terror* she had felt when she could not understand the changes imposed on her as a child. Now an adult, she was not aware of what she was doing with her therapist, but it succeeded in communicating what was so troublesome, and what she could not consciously formulate and put into words.

Unconscious communications of this kind are immensely powerful, much more so than reasonable words. The practitioner felt disorientated and as if he were the one who was mad. It was a similarly powerful message that the health visitor received from Mr Roker: 'Do not notice; do not see that I have stolen my wife's role; this is the only way that I can cope', and from Mrs Roker: 'Do not rock the boat.'

When these powerful messages affect the practitioner and he

is unable to put into words what is happening between him and his client, he is likely, without seeing what he is doing, *to display the same behaviour* to his supervisor. When the phenomenon moves one step sideways like this, we call it a 'reflection' of the transference.[5] As Searles, who first wrote about this, said:

> ... my experience in hearing numerous therapists present cases before groups has caused me to become slow in forming an unfavourable opinion of any therapist on the basis of his presentation of a case. With convincing frequency I have seen that a therapist who during an occasional presentation appears to be *lamentably* (our emphasis) anxious, confused in his thinking, or what not, actually is a basically capable colleague who, as it were, is trying unconsciously by his demeanour during the presentation to show us a major problem-area in the therapy of his patient. The problem-area is one which he cannot perceive objectively and describe to us effectively in words: rather, he is unconsciously identifying with it and is in effect trying to describe it by the way of his behaviour during the presentation.[6]

At one remove from the powerful immediacy of the therapeutic encounter, the supervisor may be freer than the practitioner to make sense of and understand some of the unconscious messages which the practitioner received and then unconsciously displays in the supervisory setting.

When cases are presented and supervised in groups, the reflection of the transference will, until it can be understood and put into words, affect the behaviour of the group. In groups, interactive processes often get 'blown-up' and the behaviour becomes more extreme than in one-to-one situations. The behaviour of the discussion group is, therefore, often a clear diagnostic aid as to what the client is trying to tell but cannot put into words, or is defending against because the feeling is too painful to hold in consciousness.

The countertransference, whether it is evoked in and identified by an individual practitioner, or reflected in the course of a group discussion, while offering important information about the client, is, by its very nature, a complex and subtle phenomenon which is not without its own limitations and dangers as a tool in the service of further understanding. We forget at our peril that the practitioner will not be so objective in his professional stance as to be free of his *own* confusion, uncertainty, anxiety, incompetence and prejudice, which may well be stimulated in the course of his involvement with the client. In the present economic climate, the employed practitioner may well have good reason to be worried and anxious about the security of his own job, or the survival of the agency which employs him. During the period of the pilot workshop in London, the IMS was under severe financial pressure with the possibility of redundancies having to be considered. We recall how difficult it was to work effectively with the practitioners on the cases of their unemployed clients, without having our own personal anxieties and worries disturbingly aroused by the nature of the case material.

The term countertransference was in fact first coined to refer to the practitioner's own emotional difficulties which could be aroused in the therapeutic relationship, and therefore distort and disturb the proper understanding of and work with the client. It is a more recent development in psychodynamic theory, following on the greater understanding of the unconscious mechanisms of projection and projective identification, that has led to the recognition that some of the feelings aroused in the practitioner may be a result of the client's unconscious but purposeful communication.

Countertransference, as a source of information about the client, can most appropriately be used when supported by other evidence from the client's history or the nature of his current social or personal relationships. With Mr and Mrs Acton, for example, the therapist working with Mrs Acton knew from his co-therapist who was seeing her husband that Mr Acton often talked about his uncomfortable feelings of losing contact with his wife and feeling that she seemed to leave him out of her thoughts and plans. The therapist also knew that when Mrs Acton first left home she lived with various friends at different addresses and her parents often did not know where to contact her. With this knowledge about Mrs Acton, which was in line with his countertransference feelings, he could assume with some confidence that these feelings were being unconsciously evoked in him by the client, rather than being a sign of his professional limitations or private problems.

For the practitioner to use his countertransference without supporting evidence is at best naive and omnipotent, and at worst it may persecute the client who will feel not only misunderstood, but also as though he were being unconsciously used by the practitioner to disown and project his own difficulties and anxieties.

With this important qualification in mind, this chapter continues to describe our feelings or defended behaviour with our clients in the IMS and in the workshops, when we and the members were affected by powerful messages from the members' clients. Sometimes our responses were initially conditioned by a particularly convincing defensive system such as that of Mr and Mrs Roker until Mrs Roker broke down in tears at the meeting at the school. Sometimes we, like the clients, needed the defence because we could not tolerate and accommodate the feelings against which such strong defences were needed. When we joined the defensive system for any undue length of time, we confirmed our clients' worst fears about themselves and their partners and their belief that nothing could change. When we could recognise our involvement in the underlying interactive system into which they had drawn us and then use our feelings creatively, we could change our stance and give the clients the means and the hope of being able to change theirs. Our involvement gave us additional information about the plight of the clients, but in this part of the book we concentrate on the practitioners.

At the beginning of the project we were aware of our own failure with some of our unemployed clients, and also that many other practitioners were not working as effectively with this group as they were with other client-groups. Was this simply because many had trained before the economic recession and had not been properly equipped to respond to the current social situation in some areas of the country? But why, we asked, when practitioners have usually been trained to help people mourn their losses, could they often not recognise loss of job as something needing to be mourned? Eventually we came to the conclusion that some of the unconscious messages and defensive systems were stronger in relation to unemployment and the grief incurred by it than in other situations of extreme stress which many practitioners take in their stride. This statement is supported by our discussion in Part II of the intensity and ambivalence of the grief and the complexity of the mourning process after loss of job, compounded as this is by the problems relating to envy.

The predominant themes we now describe in relation to employed practitioners have their source, we believe, in the practitioners' involvement, or defence against involvement, with their clients. In a process of interaction they were often more influenced by the clients than able to exert their own influence, at least until they were able to understand what was going on between them and their clients.

Blind in one eye

In the Introduction we mentioned one of the main findings of the project: 'People do not want to know about the adverse affects of unemployment.' The subject was unpopular; we had difficulty in getting funds and in collecting our clinical sample; the workshop in Tyneside was undersubscribed, despite one of the local services having 74% of its total clientele unemployed. This was probably typical of most services in that area.

Obviously those practitioners who chose to attend a workshop on unemployment were interested in the subject. None of them had been coerced into coming. As we mentioned in the Introduction, some of them, it transpired, had had personal or close experience of the situation either through their own previous unemployment or that of their spouse, child or relative. It seemed they wanted help in making sense of their own experience which, at least, helped them to empathise with their clients. They could not, therefore, be said to be a group who, overall, denied the severity of the problem nor its impact on individuals, marriages and families.

So it was surprising when members of the workshop told us that *we had invented unemployment!* A reflection? 'You lot seem to have created it', one health visitor ruefully commented on the second leg of the sandwich-workshop. She explained that on returning to her office after the first week she had looked through her case files and discovered, much to her surprise, that the majority of the families contained at least one unemployed member. Despite her interest in the subject, she had not been able to let herself know the scale of the problem in the area in which she worked and how much it affected her own caseload. Another practitioner, a probation officer, also discovered, but again only after the first week of the workshop, that 24 out of 26 clients for whom she was professionally responsible were unemployed.

Why, when the practitioners were concerned and interested enough to attend a two-week workshop, had some of them not been able to take note of the scale of the problem on their own caseloads? We do not think they were normally obtuse; but we do think they got caught up in the defensive system of many of the families with whom they worked and that they were unconsciously influenced by their clients' denial. This influence would be of considerable force if it came from not just one client, but from 24 out of 26.

Some of the painful feelings that were denied with such force were clearly those concerning loss, not just the obvious loss of the job and its manifest and latent functions, but also the loss of the particular meaning attached to that specific job as we described in Part I. In Part II we noted the ready response of some clients when the practitioners refused to join the defensive system – the lessening of the despair and self-destructive behaviour and then the renewed energy. However, the strength of the feelings in some couples which needed to be worked with if the defence was to be given up was well illustrated by one social worker on the pilot workshop in London.

In his application for this workshop he had mentioned a case with which he experienced considerable difficulty; he wanted help with this work. Yet it was only at the ninth of the ten seminars that he presented the family. His concise presentation was in accordance with his previously having been a confident, useful, clear-thinking member of the group. So why did he have to leave getting help for his own work until the 'eleventh hour'? And then only at the end of his presentation did he remember to inform the group that the previous week the husband had secured a job after two years' unemployment. He answered the leader's unspoken question: 'Why only now do you tell us?' He had not been able to present his work with this family before because their distress had been so great that they had all avoided the issue; he had therefore nothing to tell the workshop. It was only when the husband had got back into a job, that the practitioner could listen and therefore the family could speak about the detail of their previous misery.

This social worker and Mr and Mrs Roker's health visitor were just two of many practitioners who received 'Keep Off' messages: 'It is all too painful to know about.' This degree of pain is daunting, but does not, we believe, fully explain the degree to which the practitioners were affected. Many are trained in counselling skills and are able to withstand strong feelings of grief in other situations of loss. We believe they were receiving other powerful messages.

Man-made

If we use the reflection in the workshop – the blown-up, stark accusation that we, the leaders, had created unemployment and our amazement at being so accused, we may deduce that the practitioners were trying to tell us about the content and force of a message they were receiving but were unable to bring to consciousness. They did not know how accused *they* were. It seemed they were being given unconscious messages that they had created unemployment; apparently their clients felt that unemployment was man-made, not God-made. The practitioners in their employed status, however helpful they tried to be, had become a ready butt for their clients' often unvoiced fury against society – a society which was felt to be not only responsible for their unemployment, but also a society which they felt accused them of not trying hard enough to find a job. The practitioners were on the receiving end of an underlying 'belt' of hostility: 'I'm accusing you, because I feel so accused, and I want you to know what it's like; I cannot put it into words.'

In any helping process the client is likely to be more hostile to the would-be helper than many practitioners can let themselves know. No one likes to be seen as dependent or as someone who is not managing his affairs properly. Further, at a more unconscious level, the more deprived the client is, the more likely it is that he will bring negative attitudes and feelings into the transference relationship with his practitioner. In Part II of this book we described how the loss of work reactivated feelings related to early losses or deprivations – deep feelings of anger, resentment and mistrust. In the transference relationship the practitioner may become the target for these feelings, as did Mrs Acton's therapist. When the client is unemployed, the hostility is magnified because the practitioner's employment symbolises (when the feeling is unconscious) or signals (when the feeling is conscious) the very thing that has been lost. Who likes to be helped by someone who has what one wants oneself?

The object of envy

Clearly, the practitioner's employment – so obvious in the situation in which unemployed client and employed practitioner meet – is the object of envy. Not surprisingly, the envy enacted within the marriages, which we described in the last chapter, also gets directed onto the practitioner, not only because the practitioner symbolises what is wanted and envied, but also because the client is trying to communicate a major problem area which he cannot put into words.

Extreme envy (unmitigated by gratification, which in its turn leads to love and gratitude) in severely deprived people, or the defence against it, is one of the most difficult phenomena to work with in a therapeutic situation, particularly when it gets directed, as it will, onto the practitioner. It 'often lies at the root of negative therapeutic reaction and interminable treatment'.[7]

In the last chapter we used Klein's definition of envy as the primitive feelings about another person's possessing and enjoying something desirable. We emphasised two aspects of these feelings. First, the innate primitive rage that seeks only to devalue, to spoil, or even to destroy the source of what is wanted so much. If it is spoiled or no longer exists, no longer need it be envied. We guess that, when the clients' defences need to be maintained, many employed practitioners are written off as useless by many unemployed clients at the first contact. Sometimes the practitioners' efforts were spoiled by a straight rejection. Mr and Mrs Marks drew their curtains and refused to answer the doorbell. Only the vicar's persistence finally gained him re-admittance. In Chapter 4 we described Mrs Streatfield's triumphant behaviour – 'I told you so' – when she had defeated the probation officer's attempts to help. She truly bit the hand which tried to feed.

Second, if the greed arising from envy is not defended

against by spoiling, it may be defended against by attempts to rob, as we have seen in the behaviour of the husbands who stole their wives' jobs and took over all the domestic and child-care tasks. Mr Quigley's envy of his wife was described in Chapter 6. He did not steal tasks, but he tried to steal all the attention for himself. He was furious with his wife for being in hospital and, as he thought, getting all the attention and support, while he was not getting as much as he wanted from his mother. He wanted to dump the children and have his mother just for himself. Such was his desperation when he failed to achieve this and sought help from the marriage guidance council, that he managed to by-pass the waiting list and usual assessment procedure.

Normally a counsellor would involve the spouse in the marital counselling whenever possible. In this instance, the female counsellor could have tried to do this when Mrs Quigley came out of hospital. It did not happen. The counsellor, aware of Mr Quigley's deprivation (never wanted, because he was born a boy) informed the workshop that 'he needed a lot of mothering'. Mr Quigley's power of seduction was even more apparent when another member asked what was happening in the marriage. 'The marriage between Mr Quigley and me?' the counsellor spontaneously asked. The subject of the relationship between Mr and Mrs Quigley had been missing in the discussion which had all centred on Mr Quigley. The group had also been submitting to the power of his appeal.

This gifted counsellor had been robbed of her usual stance and unconsciously had responded inappropriately to the greed of Mr Quigley who, if he could not have his mother just for himself, was ensuring that he got his counsellor in that role, at least for one hour a week, to the detriment of a counselling process supposedly concerned with marriage.

With some of our unemployed clients in the IMS we were surprised to find how exploited we felt, much more so than with other clients, particularly in respect of negotiated fees. (The IMS charges for its services according to income.) Mr and Mrs Bell, for example, appropriately as it seemed at first, negotiated a free service because they were on benefit – a level of income on which the fee is waived. Yet, as the therapy progressed, accounts of Mr and Mrs Bell's activities and throw-away hints suggested that they might have had a considerable sum stashed away. The therapists' fantasies as to the size of this sum grew out of all proportion to the allusions to it, but they remained the ones feeling robbed and fairly sure that Mr and Mrs Bell could have afforded to pay a fee, even if only a small one.

Another couple, Mr and Mrs Cragge, asked for help with an air of desperation and urgency. Yet they found every possible reason why they could not attend for sessions at the offered time and then many alternative times offered to them. On the one hand, it was so reasonable that with Mr Cragge's unemployment Mrs Cragge should not jeopardise her job by asking for time off in normal working hours. On the other hand, we were offering our time, our services and our skill, and they continued to reject them, just as Mr Cragge had applied for numerous jobs, offered his services and his skill, and been turned down. They certainly let us know what that felt like.

Finally, a late evening time was reluctantly offered and grudgingly accepted. When these late sessions got under way, the two therapists found they increasingly hungered for their supper. Only on the sixth session did they learn that Mr and Mrs Cragge always ate theirs before coming, and their refusal of appointment times one or two hours earlier was nonsense in respect of the time Mrs Cragge actually finished work. Mr Cragge's satisfied belch on one occasion added insult to injury.

The reason the therapists were seduced in this way in the first instance was related to the problem of collecting the clinical sample, referred to in the Introduction. They wanted Mr and Mrs Cragge in the sample. They lost their normally tougher attitude about reasonable appointment times. However, we believe their increasing hunger as the sessions progressed was related to the unconscious demand of Mr and Mrs Cragge to be filled up, leaving the therapists emotionally empty. They were normally late diners, and even if they had finished work they would not have been eating at that time. When they became conscious of how Mr and Mrs Cragge were getting them to experience their unmanageable feelings both of emptiness and of being so exploited (Mrs Cragge, the earner, exploited by Mr Cragge, the non-earner, and Mr Cragge exploited by society), the therapists' weekly 'hunger' disappeared. It also became clearer how much Mr and Mrs Cragge had exploited each other in their marriage over the years. At a later date when they were managing their affairs and relationship better, an attempt to re-negotiate the appointment-time met with no demur and there was no problem about Mrs Cragge leaving work early one day a week.*

Deeply deprived people like Mr Quigley, Mr and Mrs Bell, and Mr and Mrs Cragge, whose experiences had never enabled them to learn about love and gratitude, often feel exceptionally empty and imagine that other people have it all for the asking. The empty person can rarely know that the other may have worked hard to achieve what he has done and to master his own destructive impulses. In the circumstances of unemployment, a severely deprived client may well fantasise that, if the practitioner really tried, he could conjure up a job. When the practitioner, who in the 1960s may have been effective in helping clients find work, now failed to do this, he would be perceived as deliberately withholding, despite the rational knowledge that practitioners cannot create jobs for the taking in areas of high unemployment. (The probation officers remained uneasy about their inability to help their clients find employment; traditionally it was a requirement of many probation orders that the probationer 'lead an honest and *industrious* life'. There was the expectation that probationers, with their officer's help, find paid work.)

The practitioner as the object of envy, whether this envy robs, or in defence against the greed, seeks to spoil or destroy, loses his more usual attentive and creative counselling skills. When insatiable greed is paramount, the practitioner often reacts inappropriately in one of two ways. Like Mr Quigley's counsellor he can be drawn into a collusive fantasy that he can meet an unreal request to make up to the client for his initial deprivation – what he feels he had a right to and never had. Or the practitioner, in fear that he will be overwhelmed by the client's emotional demands and knowing that whatever he does it will never be enough, emotionally withdraws, either consciously or unconsciously. Some of the practitioners on our

---

* Processes of interaction tend to re-affect a practitioner/writer during the act of writing. In writing about this couple, the author realised that just after writing about 'hunger' and feeling so exploited (she was one of the therapists), she got up from the typewriter to feed herself before finishing the paragraph. Replete with bacon and egg inside her, she was then able to record the outcome.

workshops had unconsciously withdrawn emotionally from their clients, had often been very busy on practical issues that the client could well have carried out for himself, and throughout had failed to sit and listen to the pain.

When the unconscious urge to spoil or destroy is paramount, the practitioner *who is able to sit and listen*, may be the one who is left feeling empty, and finds himself deprived of sensible thoughts and words. His wits appear to fly out of the window, and nothing seems worth saying. He has to struggle to keep himself engaged and can sustain himself only by his knowledge of previous experience that if he perseveres and demonstrates that he cannot be destroyed – keeps on reappearing with his chin up – that this in itself is helpful and reduces the client's fear that he will always succeed in killing off the person he wants or needs and with whom he is trying to communicate. When this reassurance finally makes itself felt, the clients, feeling safer, are able to risk allowing themselves to get closer and the consciously formed words are then less imbued with unconscious hostility. The practitioner then finds himself becoming more sensible.

The therapeutic value of this capacity to sit and listen was illustrated by one clergyman who reported in the second leg of the Tyneside workshop that the situation of Mr and Mrs Little, a couple whom he had brought for discussion with much despair three months previously, was 'much more hopeful'. On the suggestion of the group he had altered his pattern of visiting from one of crisis response to regular visits at the same time each week, 'just to talk', as he explained to them. Unsure of himself in this altered role, and probably unconsciously responding to the underlying hostility, he jokingly (?) added, 'And you won't throw me out with the dog, will you?' Mr Little drew himself up to his full height and assured the vicar that he would never do that. Amidst the chaos that had always reigned in this large problem family, the vicar remained unsure of what to do. However, unbidden by him, the children soon came to be ushered out of the room when he arrived, so that Mr and Mrs Little could talk to the vicar on their own. Mrs Little remained 'cagey' and it was difficult to 'get her to open up'. Even so, her appearance started to change, as did that of the house which became much less of a hovel. Mr Little who previously had boasted of his prowess at various activities, but always shown himself quite ineffectual, built a new fireplace ('the stones perhaps "nicked" from the churchyard') which the vicar could genuinely admire. One child became a member of 'The Tyne Terriers' band and Mr Little found himself an occupation in helping to marshal the children on and off the coach when the band travelled to its weekly competitions with other such bands, and got himself entrusted with the care of the drums. The whole family seemed lifted by 'The Saints Go Marching On'. A new warmth blossomed between Mr and Mrs Little.

When the two aspects of envy are roughly of equal force, part of the powerful unconscious message being, 'Help, give me all', the other being, 'I will spoil all your best efforts and your satisfaction in your job', the practitioner, caught between the two contradictory messages, is intellectually and emotionally immobilised until he becomes conscious of what is besetting him.

Some clients in our samples did know about their envy and hostility and openly accused the practitioners of being part of the system which had deprived them of their employment. And, as one man said to his social services practitioner, 'If it weren't for the likes of me, there wouldn't be a job for you.' They were in a minority.

For the majority, the envious hostility remained unconscious and highly defended. Strong defensive systems are compelling in their unconscious invitation to others to 'get in on the act'. In general terms, the more rigid the defence, the more precarious it is and the greater the underlying emotional turmoil. Appropriately, practitioners should be careful in disturbing the system with some clients, unless they are confident they can remain on the scene (for example, not going on holiday the next week or just about to leave the job) and are emotionally robust enough to bear the uncovered feelings. With other clients, they are given little opportunity; strong defences form 'a powerful obstacle to take in'[8] what is on offer, as if the offering is distrusted and, therefore, only to be feared.

As described in Part II, denial is often used as a defence against unbearable feelings connected with loss. It is also one of the most usual defences brought into use against envy. Strong denial is often accompanied by what we call 'acting-out' – sometimes manic, often self-destructive activity used as a release of tension built up by the force of the impulse in its battle against the defence. Most practitioners would agree that 'actors-out' are among the most difficult to help. The initial engagement takes on the character of a chase, the practitioner several metres behind and hardly able to catch up with the next crisis, still so busy dealing with the previous one. Two other defences are often used against envy. One is idealisation; the exalted person becomes beyond comparison. However, this does not serve very long and sets in train a vicious circle of even more envy and then even more idealisation.[9] The other is projective identification. The envious impulse to steal, spoil or devalue can be projected into another person and that person is then seen as possessing those impulses. In the counselling relationship, the practitioner is perceived as the thief or spoiler, and the client his victim. This factor intensifies the underlying accusations that the practitioners have created unemployment which we mentioned earlier in this chapter.

No wonder then that practitioners faced with clients who act out, deny, idealise, and unconsciously seek to rob or spoil, or fear that they will be robbed or spoiled, feel at best inadequate, or at worst impotent. These defensive systems, and the unconscious messages contained in them, are particularly immobilising when they meet a similar need in the practitioner to defend against his own feelings connected with the same issue. We believe that practitioners are unduly influenced by their unemployed clients and the defensive systems which they are invited to join, because of *their* feelings about *their* employment.

The divide

If envy is a difficult feeling for anyone to manage, so too is the feeling of being envied. In the Tyneside workshop, members spoke of their problems in this respect. They parked their new cars round the corner, out of sight of the clients. As is usual, they told their clients when they were going on *leave*, a less emotive word than holiday. They were not questioned about this nor wished a 'good time', and they did not add that they were going to Majorca, as would often have happened in the past. It was as if they tried not to 'flaunt' (the word they used) the advantages and opportunities available to them through their earning power. Many other groups of clients might well not enjoy such opportunities, but, less envious, would feel less deprived and angry. The differences in these circumstances were that both clients and practitioners felt that unemployment was man-made and were aware of the increasing divide between employed and unemployed, rich and poor.

The widening gulf between the *over*-employed and the unemployed was enacted at one of the workshops. On the second leg of the sandwich, some members failed to return. This fact has to be set against the knowledge that on other IMS sandwich courses and workshops the members normally return for the next part of the event; only exceptional circumstances appear to prevent the odd person from doing so. We are experienced teachers and can normally hold a course through to its completion. We were amazed at the absenteeism, and of the sheer discourtesy in not letting us know and in not apologising. Yet, on the other hand, several of the members who had returned in what was the month of January should probably not have done so if they had had proper regard for their health. They had climbed out of sick beds, braved icy roads over long distances, and then worked prodigiously hard in the discussion groups, scarves wrapped round sore throats and aching heads, cushions supporting severely painful backs and lozenges passed round the groups. Was this indicative of the stress of the job when they were more open to hearing the clients' feelings? Along with other fitter members, they reported on the work they had done in the intervening three months since we had last met, and clearly showed how they had been able to use the fruits of the previous discussion. On the one hand, never had a workshop shown so much good work; on the other hand, it now had its sub-group of absentees, that is, its own unemployed section.

Furthering the divide is the employed person's envy of the unemployed, particularly when the employed is over-worked and the job is not satisfying. We first drew attention to this in Chapter 7 and suggested that the employed may well imagine that all the unemployed enjoy themselves in bed in the afternoons, perhaps not knowing that some of the less adjusted may well have become impotent. Even if the employed would not really like to be unemployed, they would often like a few more afternoons off. Given the poverty of many of the unemployed, it is not reasonable to think such thoughts. Envy is rarely reasonable. Can the employed practitioner know about his own unreasonable envy, so that it does not further blunt his response?

It is often not recognised that even at the best of times practitioners can also be envious of all the help their clients receive from them and from other practitioners. They themselves have often been hurt and deprived and, constructively or not, use their occupation of helping others to help themselves. 'The doctor knows – or should know – that he does not choose this career by chance.'[10] (We refer the reader back to Part I.) This is why practitioners are usually more effective with patients and clients whose inner preoccupations are psychologically similar to their own in that they are prepared to engage with the client in the struggle (as long as they themselves are consciously in touch with their own preoccupation and continue to remind themselves of the differences as well as the similarities between them).

If a practitioner cannot own his own envy, he fails to recognise the signs in others and is, therefore, less creative with seriously envious clients. We wonder whether practitioners are less effective with their unemployed clients, more emotionally withdrawn from them than they would be with other clients, because of their own unrecognised envy of the supposed delightful leisure their clients might be enjoying. To be oneself the object of envy, and envious in return is, to put it mildly, a basis for a divisive relationship.

The expression of anger

In reflecting on this image of the divide, an increasingly familiar image in the present social and economic climate, the practitioners shared with each other their social and political awareness. For some, this led to the expression of feelings of guilt and shame – guilt and shame about the psychological and material benefits accruing from their employment in contrast to the deprivation and disadvantage of the unemployed, some of whom were their clients. They wondered how this might affect their professional practice. Some practitioners said that sometimes they wished that the unemployed would be more outspoken about their sense of deprivation and frustration, even if this meant political protest and rebellion. It was as if they felt that such an expression of anger by the unemployed was preferable to the self-defeating and immobilising feelings of personal despair and hopelessness which they as practitioners had to deal with in their work with these clients.

This led to the practitioners becoming aware of another set of feelings: their fear of their clients' rage, which if unleashed might lead to violence and anarchy. If they helped their clients to get in touch with their feeling of anger, be it that inherent in loss, or that attached to envy, would they be *inciting* violence in the family or the community? As we noted in Chapter 5, statistically, unemployed husbands are more likely to be divorced for intolerable behaviour than employed husbands; and the factor of unemployment is often recorded in families in which child abuse occurs.

Further, as one of the practitioners asked, if *all* the practitioners in an area of high unemployment helped *all* their clients to acknowledge their anger, would they then be fuelling the possibility of anarchy and riot? This fear became particularly conscious in the second week of the workshop in Tyneside, an inner city area which, like many others, contains much of the deprivation and despair which may lead to community disintegration and socially destructive behaviour.

'A bit extreme?' the reader may think. Perhaps, but the Tyneside practitioners were, we believe, carrying their own political and social anger; their anger that sometimes they seemed to be so useless in their work with these clients who really needed a job which they could not give them; and, in addition, they carried the projected anger of some of their clients. In carrying their own angry feelings and those of their clients (x24 [or the number of unemployed clients on their case load]), they would be particularly fearful about the outcome of this amount of anger. Would they incite social violence, they asked, or would this anger be directed against them personally as embodiments of the system which appears to frustrate and deprive? This notion is not so irrational in terms of recent cases of rape, bodily harm and even murder inflicted on social workers and other practitioners.

Perhaps it was this fear of uncontainable anger, unconscious for many of us until we discussed it together, that partly explained why these practitioners, many of whom would normally be able to help their clients get in touch with the usual feelings of grief after bereavement or other personal loss, defend themselves against these feelings as much as the clients do, when the loss is that of a job. The reader may remember the GP referred to in the introduction who, although working in an East End borough of London, stoutly maintained that he had no unemployed patients on his list.

The other part of the explanation may be to do with the powerful feelings attached to envy, or the defence against these feelings. Little did we realise when we embarked on this project – and how naive could we be (we are four experienced therapists) – that we would be writing a book in which the most significant and overriding theme in the material was that of *envy*, envying and being envied, and not wanting to know about it, just as in the beginning we were not able to know.

It is as though, in the context of the primitive feelings aroused by loss and envy which we have described, the client *and* the practitioner get mutually caught up in an unconscious and collusive belief that these feelings, if made more conscious, could not be managed and contained, and would only be expressed in a highly destructive way. It may be this anxiety which prevents both clients and practitioners keeping sight of the fact that anger and frustration can also be harnessed into constructive and creative action. By definition, creativity and construction can only come about through the positive expression and use of potency and aggression.

In referring to creativity and construction, we are talking about growth, development and change. Change involves the giving up of the old to make room for the new, and requires a process of mourning for that which has been lost, or has had to be given up. Included in this mourning process is the management of the feelings of anger associated with loss and, if these angry feelings are avoided, mourning will be incomplete. The possibility of development and change will then be inhibited. The bereaved person, whatever the nature of the loss, be it a loved one or a job, will remain immobilised or at least limited in his capacity to move on.

However, this process of change, which includes a mourning for that which has been lost, depends on an environment which facilitates its management and realisation by offering support, containment, opportunity and hope. This is as true of social change as of individual development. In the same way as a new-born infant needs the facilitating environment of his family, so social change is dependent on cultural and political structures which support and promote that change.

If this is the case, as we believe it is, then the therapeutic relationship between the practitioner and his unemployed client can only be *fully* examined and understood within the broader social, political and economic context (environment) in which it takes place. Employment and unemployment are social, economic and political features of our culture, as well as being factors in the life of an individual and his family. Using the word 'political' in the broadest sense, it is this simultaneously personal and political nature of employment and unemployment that we examine in the next chapter.

9

The Management of Change

... getting out of the tramlines of tradition is not easy ...
Bill Jordan, President
Amalgamated Engineering Union

It's a funny thing work, isn't it? It's the sort of central pivot that most of us that are in work live around, and we then make social pariahs out of people who don't work.

Amanda Maddock

The turbulent environment

While we were working on this project we found it impossible to divorce our professional from our political selves. In 1954 Titmuss wrote, 'The worker, the client and the setting are basic components of actions and must be viewed as a whole.'[1] He was referring to the institutional setting which legitimises and supports the practitioner in his professional relationships with his clients. The tripartite whole exists within the larger political, economic, social and value systems, all of which exert a powerful influence on each other and on setting, worker and client.

Clients and practitioners view economic and social phenomena through different coloured spectacles. A particular political philosophy affects practitioners' attitudes to their clients, just as clients' views affect what sort of help they believe they have a right to expect. Changes in benefit rates to the unemployed and other disadvantaged groups, and reduction or increase in central or local government funding affect resources of and demands on services and the efficiency with which they are delivered.

In contrast to the view that unemployment is 'like famine or floods ... coming to be seen as an act of God, a painful disaster

175

about which little can be done',[2] the practitioners with whom we worked saw unemployment as 'man-made' and, unlike famine and flood, bereavement or handicap, as something that could have been avoided; it was a political, economic and social fact as well as a personal and private matter for their clients and millions of other people (the exact number much disputed). Many spoke of their belief that politicians could wield influence in reducing the level if they chose to do so. Some politicians believe likewise. In the campaign for the General Election in June 1987, the view prevailed in the Conservative Party that its efforts would reduce the number of unemployed by 900,000 in three years; the Labour Party planned to cut it by one million in two years; and the Alliance parties aimed to do the same in three years.

However, during the campaign a national newspaper asked, 'Where all the jobs are supposed to come from'.[3] As the number of people of working age increase as the century moves into its last decade, about 250,000 jobs will need to be created for the unemployment figure to remain level[4] and recent projections indicate little real growth in employment up to the end of this decade. One study suggests that about 500,000 jobs in the service sector could be created by 1990 against a projected loss of 650,000 jobs in other areas of the economy;[5] that at present, growth in small businesses is more than counteracted by reductions in large companies; and suggests that overall the labour force will fall slightly, but that its composition will be radically altered with even more women doing more part-time temporary work than at present. The National Institute of Economic and Social Research predicts that the recent fall in the number of unemployed will continue during the year 1987, flatten out at 2.9 million in 1988 and then climb back to three million in 1989 and 3.1 million in 1991.[6] In the shadow of these statistics are the spouses and dependent children increasing the number affected by several more millions.

Whatever the reliability of these forecasts (and the figures get hotly contended as one political party accuses another of 'massaging' them to disguise the true picture), large scale production of goods in this country continues to wane and ever more sophisticated technologies continue to reduce and redistribute the number of employees required in many industries and businesses. As computers take over in offices and factories, and service jobs increase, there is an inevitable restructuring of patterns of employment. The country has started to move into what has been called the 'post-industrial'[7] phase. This has been defined as a situation in which the new technologies no longer absorb the bulk of the energies of the employable population.[8] Although fully developed post-industrialism is still a long way off, the country is in the throes of a massive transition, perhaps the most significant disruption of the world of work and employment since the Industrial Revolution and, once started, seemingly inevitable and unstoppable.

This particular transition accompanies other big social changes. 'Emphasis is no longer on minimum standards for health and growth, but on the realisation of potential both for the individual and society.'[9] As we noted in Chapter 2, we have moved into an 'Age of Psychology', and also into an age of increased emphasis on consumerism, and built-in obsolescence and expendability of goods. In some regions and sub-cultures, social class and marital roles have become less clearly defined and structured compared with the first half of the century. In Chapter 3 we commented on the new emphasis on comradeship in marriage with an accompanying unfulfilled ideology of egalitarianism, and a sharply rising divorce rate. Marriage has never been more criticised as an institution, yet it remains remarkably popular and, despite personal failure in one marriage, people continue to marry a second or even a third time. As Toffler in his book, *Future Shock*, suggests, attitudes to the expendability of consumer goods have spread to human relationships,[10] but as Sutherland points out, this 'does not appear to be adaptive for personal growth and development'.[11]

There are immense contradictions within these changed attitudes, as there are in respect of the expectation of future employment, its form and its valuation. While the employment statistics quoted above indicate there will not be enough jobs for some considerable time, political pronouncements promise otherwise: 'Jobs will be available in the service sector, small firms and by regional assistance programmes' (Conservative); 'in the public and private sector' (Labour); 'in building and repair work' (Alliance). In respect of unemployment, a policy of tighter control of benefits to 'combat the "Why work" syndrome', suggests that the party in power finds it necessary to continue to uphold a work ethic. However, a recent study indicates a lessening of its espousal among the workforce in Britain, more so than in any other of the eight countries included in the study.[12]

We are speaking of a 'turbulent' environment, characterised by increased levels of complexity, interdependence and relevant uncertainty.[13] Turbulence arises in a system because of an accelerating but uneven rate of change in the constituent sub-systems and because of unpredictable connections between them. More and more of the goods we now consume are produced abroad, different parts of these goods often manufactured in different countries and assembled in yet another before being imported. Most of the biggest industries in this country are multi-national firms. We can be affected economically in this country by war between Arab States in the Middle East, by change of leadership in another country or by revolution in some far-off island which we may never have heard of before. Within *seconds* the Stock Exchange in Britain can be influenced by price movements in Japan. Desecration of forests or pollution in one part of the world affects climate and production in other parts. Sweden blames Britain for its acid rain. Production of lamb was affected in Wales and north west England following human error and subsequent nuclear disaster in Chernobyl, Russia.

With this increased 'knock-on' effect throughout the world, with new and wider perceptions and accompanying, but often lagging, shifts in attitudes and values, it is sometimes difficult to know what is fact and what is fiction. There is often discrepancy between what is thought to be happening and what is actually happening at different levels of the system, so that what we hear said does not match up with our personal experience. Familiar patterns of relating are disturbed. No longer can one rely on looking around for a clear-cut model of behaviour. Uncertainty, diversity, contradiction and disjunction are the norm.

Our society has a problem in how to manage this turbulence and disjunction and in how to contain the high level of anxiety consequent on the social and psychological disruption for the community and the individuals who comprise it. An accelerated but uneven rate of change poses 'far reaching problems concerning the limits of human adaptation'.[14]

The problem of change and the collective defence

Earlier in this book we described the defences used by individuals to protect themselves against anxiety and the weight of grief concordant with the number of changes and losses incurred by redundancy. Unable to move through their grief (as also reported in other studies), impeded by poverty and powerlessness, and consumed with envy, they were not able to make a creative adaptation to the changes imposed on them. We also described how, for example, in a marriage, the defences of one partner could be used by the other or, in a splitting process, be shared between them, thus forming a mutual defensive system. This process can extend itself into a large group phenomenon, and just as we cannot ignore the impact of economic and social forces on individuals, marriages and families, similarly we cannot ignore the influence of psychological forces on social customs and institutions. In 1913 Freud wrote about the connection:

> Our knowledge of the neurotic illnesses of individuals has been of much assistance to our understanding of the great social institutions. For the neuroses themselves have turned out to be attempts to find individual solutions for the problems of compensating for unsatisfied wishes, while the institutions seek to provide social solutions for the same problem.[15]

Jung made a similar statement:

> ... the apparently individual conflict of the patient is revealed as a universal conflict of his environment and epoch. Neurosis is thus nothing less than an individual attempt, however unsuccessful, to solve a universal problem.[16]

More recently Jacques and Menzies have described how groups of people in institutions develop defences to deal with potentially disruptive anxiety in the same way that individuals employ defences to ward off unmanageable feelings.[17] In Chapter 2 we referred to this, when we spoke in connection with the nursing profession, of the defensive system of the individual needing to be roughly consistent with the group defensive system established by the previous generation in an organisation. Only then would satisfaction of individual workers outweigh dissatisfaction in the job.

Primary defences used by individuals become institutionalised by the collective process. In these terms society as a whole exhibits not only its inherent conflicts, but also defences against the anxiety these conflicts arouse. For example, on the one hand it promotes the development and benefits of the new technology (and is unable to put the clock back), yet at the same time it is apparently fearful of the process of change and continues vigorously to promote the virtues of employment and a work oriented culture, ignoring many of the social repercussions of large-scale unemployment and giving little of much needed attention to alternative creative uses of time.

The period of transition is like a 'No man's land' (as it probably felt during the Industrial Revolution), old habits and ways of thought no longer appropriate, new ways not yet established and accommodated, and the future remaining uncertain. In these situations some degree of anxiety is inevitable for citizens, leaders and rulers. Given the nature of man and the degree of change needing to be encompassed, some defensive behaviour is, we believe, inevitable. As Marris says, resistance to change needs to be respected. It cannot be explained away just as 'ignorance, failure of nerve, the obstinate protection of untenable privileges ... as if the resistance could be broken by its irrationality.'[18] As he says,

> The impulse to defend the predictability of life is a fundamental and universal principle of human psychology. Conservatism, in this sense, is an aspect of our ability to survive in any situation; for without continuity we cannot interpret what events mean to us, nor explore new kinds of experience with confidence.

Required adaptation to change can occur only when the new experience can be placed in relationship to what in the past has been a familiar and generally recognised reality. For the employed and unemployed, employment has been a familiar reality. Within this context of conservatism, the collective defences which came to our attention during the course of the project were denial, splitting and projection (described in earlier chapters in respect of individuals and partners in marriage).

These defences are usually considered to be of the more

primitive type, originating earlier in the developmental process than many others. We suggest that it is these defences, rather than more sophisticated ones, that come into play because of the degree of primitive anxiety that is aroused by loss, or threat of loss, of job. The anxiety is so primitive because, since the beginning of human life, work (as opposed to employment) – use of hand, eye and brain – has been connected in the mind with physical survival, and therefore, with psychological stability.

The collective denial

The reader may remember our first main finding reported in the Introduction: people do not want to know about the reality of the psychological impact of unemployment on others. Denial was one of the most commonly used defences against the unpalatable truth. We found that patients and clients often did not declare their unemployment and the practitioners did not ask the vital questions which would elicit the particular impact for an individual or a family. We also experienced this denial in our search for funding. One Trust which refused a grant for the project on the implications of unemployment said it would have been interested and would have considered the request within its rubric if the research came up with answers as to how unemployment could be prevented.

Throughout this book we have quoted studies and figures which indicated, for example, a relationship on the one hand between ill-health, suicide, para-suicide, divorce and poverty, and on the other hand unemployment. However, there is a general paucity of research on this subject. In 1986 Laurance wrote, 'More than five years after unemployment began its dramatic rise, the lack of high quality research on the subject is striking.'[19] And Smith, writing the previous year, stated:

> If I stop to think of the amount published on, for instance, hypertension or cancer of the colon I can only conclude that doctors and medical researchers have shamefully neglected the study of how unemployment harms the health of families.[20]

Laurance also reported on the DHSS putting pressure on the Central Statistical Office to have a table on unemployment and health removed from that year's issue of *Social Trends*.[21]

Again in the same year, Veitch drew attention to the delay in publication of a politically sensitive report which plotted the link between poverty, unemployment and death rates from 1979 to 1983.[22] The plight of the unemployed, it seemed, was to remain in the shadow of public knowledge. The unpalatable, the unpopular, the unmanageable, the politically uncomfortable was not to be faced.

In the election campaign of 1987 the existence of the unemployed was not denied by any party. Employment/ unemployment was one of the main issues, but the emphasis remained on the conservative retention of the familiar. The familiar was jobs – new jobs after loss of old jobs. By only promising more jobs, the reality of long-term unemployment was denied. No party suggested that there needed to be a complete review of the whole subject. In addition, between them, the parties courted wage earners with promises of continuing cuts in taxation, the ill with a better Health Service, the pensioner with better benefits. The plight of the unemployed, their poverty and their frustration remained largely ignored.

In all these examples, the corporate defence was that of denying existing realities. There was a negation of economic and social change, and apparent refusal to recognise the manifest failure of the market to provide full employment now or in the immediate future.

The collective split and projection

Along with the over-use of denial, splitting is another defence commonly used against anxiety produced by conflicting feelings. In Chapter 3 we illustrated how a couple could externalise their mutual internal conflict by one partner expressing one set of feelings for them both, the other partner left to express the opposing set – the desire to attack expressed by one, and the desire to placate and keep impotent by the other. In Chapter 5 we described how the contrary feelings of sadness and anger inherent in grief could be divided between equally grief stricken partners.

When change is inevitable, this type of split can be enacted by one partner firmly espousing the change, the other firmly resisting it and, just as we described in Chapter 3, the one who promotes the change need not know about his or her resistance as long as the other is expressing this for him. Fowles illustrated this phenomenon in his novel, *Daniel Martin*: the wife, Jane, in describing her arid marriage attributed all the resistance against change to her 'innocent' husband, Anthony; their daughter, Rosalind, in speaking of her mother after Anthony's death, could see, 'That's just her problem ... not changing. In spite of all her talk about it.'[23]

In a change from old to new patterns of work, the split between changers and resisters of change at a group or social level is often enacted in long-fought-out struggles, particularly when it is felt that change is to be imposed by management without adequate consultation with the workers who will be affected. In recent years, miners, printers and teachers have participated in such struggles. In 1984/85 the miners in a 12-month strike resisted the threatened closure of uneconomic pits; they fought not just for their jobs, but even more fiercely for the maintenance of their communities. Following their defeat, a more recent strike ostensibly concerned with work practices and disciplinary measures was, it has been suggested, more to do with 'things altogether more timeless – hurt pride and revenge'.[24] In 1986 the printers' union resisted through violent picketing the introduction of new less labour-intensive technologies which could be managed by other tradesmen on an alternative site. They also fought for their jobs and for the power the union had previously held. Over several years teachers have protested loudly through sporadic strikes, initially for higher salaries, latterly in protest against loss of negotiating rights and changes proposed for the profession by the Government.

In these prolonged struggles it often becomes unclear what were the basic complaints underlying the protest other than that there must be no change. In this type of fight, each side becomes more entrenched in its stance (even if the basis of the stance is not clear). And each side becomes less able to hear the point of view of the other as it fights to maintain its own power and, therefore, the means to dominate and manipulate the other side. The ill-treatment of the resisters of change becomes more flagrant, as the frustration in the face of the inevitable becomes more violent in its expression. Modern technologies which have extended the means and speeded up the rate of communications have far outstripped people's ability to try to understand each other in the complex processes of rapid social change and in the face of the natural anxiety it arouses.

These strikes failed to achieve their overt aims. Many miners and printers are now unemployed. The type of split we have described gets further enacted between employed and unemployed groups. In the last chapter we wrote about the divide between unemployed clients and employed practitioners, the corporate envy of each group of the other accentuating the divide. In Chapter 2 we noted how the employed now often work for longer hours than previously, sometimes with two jobs and also working on their own homes, while those who are unemployed rarely have enough money to work at all, either on their homes, providing their own subsistence in allotment or garden, or on hobbies or other pastimes.

How difficult it is for the often over-employed not to split off the unemployed from meaningful activity was vividly illustrated for us by the experience in one of the day centres which we visited in the course of our project. The centre offered a variety of services and activities for the unemployed in the local community. It was run by a small dedicated staff group. It was the users of the centre, not the staff, who eventually suggested that there should be a users' committee which should have representation on the management committee. The staff agreed to this suggestion which was duly put into effect.

One of the first complaints the users' representative brought to the attention of the management committee was that users perceived the staff as 'restrictive, controlling and remote'. Tension focussed on the running of the coffee bar which was manned by staff. Why, the users asked, could they not run the bar? Why did the staff monopolise all the work, responsibility and status? Whereas the users protested about their lack of meaningful activity, the staff perceived the users as not having the necessary commitment and they, after all, were the ones paid to do the work. After prolonged debate, the users won the day.

However the process then repeated itself. The users who first took over the coffee bar refused to share the responsibility with others who became interested. The users running the bar were the ones now seen as 'restrictive, remote and monopolising'. It was as if runners and non-runners awarded the status of work to the runners who drew upon themselves the envy and anger of those who still did not have a job and felt deprived by those who did. There was, in effect, man-made unemployment within the centre.

A similar phenomenon had occurred earlier in the life of the centre. Soon after its establishment, the 'in-group' of earliest members attempted to restrict the more recently unemployed from joining. Feelings ran so high that physical fights ensued. The belongers, it seemed, had to find a group to carry the discomfort and anxiety inherent in their own situation in an attempt to enhance their own precarious sense of comfort and cohesion.

History has consistently demonstrated that the majority in its own self-interest uses minority groups not only to carry extreme hardship for the total culture, but also as a vehicle for the projections of the majority of all that is bad, negligent and dissolute. However these groups, usually identifiable by one or more distinctive features, such as race, religion or ethnic background, usually share a common heritage and display much cohesiveness. In fighting for equality with the majority and for better treatment, they show little desire to leave the ranks of their own minority group. By contrast, the unemployed state is still seen as transitory and the unemployed person is defined only by what he is not. In a work-centred society, unemployment is a negative reference.

The negative definition of what they are not is accentuated by the collective judgement of what they – the unemployed – must not have. Benefit remains minimal and has become more tightly and suspiciously controlled. It is notable – perhaps it always has been – that abuse of benefit by the unemployed attracts far more public attention than tax avoidance (even evasion) which is sometimes openly admired.

87% of the population of working age – the employed majority – have experienced their standard of living rising faster in the 1980s than in the 1970s. During this last decade the property-owning classes have swollen as people have bought their council houses and shares in de-nationalised industries at knock-down prices. In 1987 40% of the population chose to put back into power the party which over the previous eight years had helped them to achieve standards and heightened their expectations. This party had been seen to strengthen the economy and cut the rate of inflation and in doing so promoted a liberal policy of free enterprise, the virtues of rugged individualism (as opposed to cosy paternalism), fending for self, autonomy and increase of options for the individual by the promotion of private services alongside those owned and managed by the state.

The concept of options, as defined by Dahrendorf, as 'structured opportunities for choice to which individual choice or decisions correspond',[25] is dear to the heart of the liberal thinker. Increased options offer more life chances and, as he said, 'Societies called modern have brought an enormous increase in human life chances, greater perhaps than that wrought by any other theme in history.'

Yet in the promotion of options and choices by the present government, it is the loss of these options which so mightily affects the unemployed. Choice is never literally free of external or internal constraints for the employed, but the realm of choice is much more severely impaired for those on unemployment benefit. Along with other disadvantaged groups on benefit, the majority of the unemployed are caught in a poverty trap in which their autonomy is severely limited compared with the rest of the population; often there is no way out – no option to be in or out.

A government which, on the one hand, vigorously promotes autonomy and choice, has at the same time left recipients of state benefit in a dependent and passive position, unable to affect their own lives or those of others. And further, it is now introducing a shift away from unconditional benefit by an insistence on compulsory enrolment on various Manpower Services schemes. The availability test for unemployment and supplementary benefit is becoming more stringent. There are compulsory 'Re-start' interviews for all long-term unemployed. The government is considering making young people ineligible for benefit if they refuse places on youth training schemes and may extend this compulsion to community programmes and job training schemes. By expanding the number of schemes, making them compulsory, and constantly re-cycling the unemployed through them, it hopes to reduce unemployment.

However, much of the work that is offered on these schemes,

particularly community programmes, is deliberately marginal and of low productivity – giant occupational therapy – and, as some young people have said, has left them less fitted for the real world of employment than previously. Compulsory schemes such as these mirror employment in Russia – coercive, under threat, over-manned and low waged – the exact opposite of the policy which promotes autonomy and options. The fear of affording more choice to underprivileged unemployed people arises, we suspect, from the fantasy that, if given more freedom of choice, they would then attack the power base of the privileged.

The one idea that does not get debated or promoted publicly by any party is whether in an era when there are not enough jobs for everyone now nor likely to be for the foreseeable future, people should be allowed the autonomy to choose to work or not to work. Promotion and discussion of social dividend schemes, not a modern idea, whereby, for example, the State provides every individual with an income sufficient to relieve him of the compulsion to work but in a position to improve his income[26] remain in learned tomes and behind closed doors.

The change required in values and attitudes is apparently too big, too shocking, too threatening to be contemplated in a wider arena, despite the claim that 'without greatly increasing taxes on earnings from all sources' the redistribution of income would be 'relatively simple'.[27] As Jordan argues,

> The mechanism of the social dividend which replaces tax allowances and social security benefits by a universal unconditional weekly payment by the State to every citizen does not violate the essential principle of liberalism. It does not attempt to impinge any pattern on the final outcome of production and exchange. It allows every individual rather than property holders alone, to have the maximum choice in what they do, what they earn, what they sell and what they give away. It accepts the outcome of these decisions as being the optimum, and does not force anyone to do or be what they don't want to do or be. All the State does is to tax everyone with an income and redistribute an equal share of the proceeds to everyone, whether they have an income or not.[28]

However the opportunity and then the need to make decisions between options can be as paralysing as lack of options. A pilot project to test the validity of the modern burden of choice showed that most respondents were bewildered, sensing that there were more options open to them than they recognised; they had difficulty in obtaining and sifting relevant information, and in predicting the implications of different courses of action; some respondents commented on their lack of a solid core of values to guide them in their choices.[29] Progress, it can be said, is never a one way street.

On our theme of the collective split, it is as if the divide between those able to choose and encouraged to be autonomous, and those kept firmly in a position in which they have no choice is maintained (obviously) by the choosers to keep at bay their own anxiety inherent in the burden of choice. It can be easier and, therefore, enviable to be able to say 'I had no choice, I had to do it' than 'I didn't know what to do and then I decided to ...'. The ability to make choices requires some maturity. For some people, the discomfort of choosing is more problematic than the disheartening situation of having no choice. When there is denial of the problems that choice brings in its wake, accentuated as these are the more complex society becomes, the discomfort and guilt about being in this position has to get projected and located in those who have no opportunity for choice; they, the unemployed, are then seen as workshy and having, by their own default, chosen their present plight.

We believe this split is maintained so prodigiously because it clearly suits the majority to look after their own interests and because of their fear of attack on those interests. It is an example of what Kant called the 'antagonism' within society – the 'unsocial sociability' of man or his ambivalence about being a social creature; on the one hand he recognises his inclination and basic need to be sociable; on the other hand, he has a 'persistent resistance which permanently threatens to disrupt society'.[30]

Ill-fare or welfare?

One of the options open to any modern society is the concept of welfare it chooses to adopt. Welfare is defined in the *Concise Oxford Dictionary* as 'Satisfactory state, health and prosperity (usually of person or society); maintenance of members of community in such condition, especially by statutory procedure or social effort.'

The last two centuries have seen a massive increase in state welfare measures, remedial, preventive and developmental, in respect of the community at large and of groups of needy individuals – the young, the old, the handicapped and disabled requiring welfare for their ill-fare. State welfare, it seems, is a function of economic and social development in that it has arisen and extended its range in response to economic and social change. At different times the state has been forced to cover the costs of change. For example, the Elizabethan Poor Law was introduced after the enclosure of common land created a class of unemployed – the 'sturdy beggars', as they were called – a new category of displaced people who no longer were the responsibility of the feudal lord. The growth of urbanised industrial environments forced the government of that time into preventive welfare such as provision of a sanitation and sewage system and other public health measures. Growth in the population and its new densities in towns necessitated a police force and a fire service. Out of industrialism, the increased amount of waged labour and lack of other means of subsistence, grew the concept of social security and insurance against dire poverty in illness and old age.

In developmental terms, industrial employment demanded a minimum standard of literacy. The 1870 Elementary Education Act which provided state primary education was the first of a series which slowly extended the school leaving age and increased provision of higher education. The growth of public libraries at the beginning of the century, followed by parks, playgrounds, sports stadia and more recently leisure centres have reflected changes in social expectations in the hierarchy of need and new values concerning the use not only of work and learning, but also of leisure.

Along with the growth in preventive and developmental facilities, the state has been required to share in the provision of, or take over remedial services pioneered by the church, lay charities, philanthropists and social reformers. For example, the probation service was formed after the early work of the police court missionaries was accepted as a necessary adjunct of the penal system. A state comprehensive child care service was instituted as part of a massive programme of social reform after the last world war when it became clear that the work of Dr Barnardo and the Waifs and Strays Society and the remnants of the old Poor Law system were not meeting the extensive need.

The reformed remedial services carried ideals of a personalised approach to individual problems. The emphasis in the newly established training and professionalism of large numbers of social workers was on personal casework with the individual client, and psychology was seen to be one of the most important subjects of study.

The welfare state which came into being as part of the programme of social reform extended ideas of social justice and a universal right to a minimum standard of living. It was backed by a comprehensive national insurance scheme from which people could not opt out, and by an *expectation of full employment*.

However, critics of the welfare state have increasingly argued over the years not only against the escalating costs and the diversion of resources from defence and wealth producing activities, but also on the emphasis on goods and the demoralising effect of reduced incentives. The argument was summarised in the sentence, 'An over-stuffed Welfare State becomes a National Featherbed.'

In line with its promotion of greater economic efficiency and of private enterprise, the present government has de-nationalised or cut back (in real financial terms) some of the previously established preventive, remedial and develop-mental welfare services. The individual consumer of average or limited means has been encouraged, often for the first time in his life, to become a shareholder in a public company. Grants for higher education have been cut, universities expected to earn more of their income or find subsidy from private sources, notably industry. Private philanthropy by the waged and salaried earners is encouraged by a new scheme of pay-roll giving. Options – state or private schemes – are being extended in the field of insurance, education, and health services.

In the midst of a process of social change, not surprisingly, the concept of welfare is changing along with the economy, as it has done in the past. Now, as in the past, the social situation is increasingly being expected to be as self-regulatory as the economy over and above a very basic minimal standard which has been reduced in real terms, so that once more many people are living below a generally accepted poverty line.

Without disagreeing with some of the recent changes, we share a concern with many other people that although the concept of welfare is changing, it is doing so in a passive and defensive way, and not taking sufficient account of the process and rate of change, and of new social injustices. History has shown that the social system is not self-regulatory at the standard which has come to be expected, and the less favourably the habitat changes, the more the state has to intervene. There is no reason to suppose that this trend will alter. In view of the increasing complexity and interdependence of world affairs, there is every reason to suppose that services will continue to be needed, but not necessarily as in the past. In fact, they will need to be as adaptive as the individual is increasingly asked to be.

This is not to suggest that we believe in endless 'feather bedding' with showers of material goods for all and sundry, although obviously we are appalled at the number of people living below the poverty line and think that, at least, benefit rates should be raised; at most, a much more equitable system of distribution of national resources should be devised.

We go further, and suggest that a modern concept of welfare, in tune with present social and economic conditions, needs to be much more active than in the past in its developmental function; that it should be more generally recognised that the best welfare is that which promotes development[31] of the individual and of the community in which he lives. In a post-industrial society, as in an industrial or any other one, the main resource is its people and their ability, or potential ability, to create a meaningful existence for themselves and others. Rather than just relieving distress, welfare actively needs to reclaim and enhance the individual's capacity, not only to function, but to adapt to a changing social world.

The system of welfare which we have inherited from the last two hundred years has supported and been controlled by an image of industrial man who is employed outside his own home. The welfare which we now need requires a recognition that society is changing, that social costs are overtaking market costs, that a new type of social balance must be struck if the new order of complexity is to be regulated, and that in this social order individualistic values of industrialism will be less pronounced.

Welfare, as Jordan[32] suggests, should not now be based, as our present National Insurance scheme is, on employment-related benefits nor on the assumption that the majority of households consist of one employed husband and one unpaid help-meet wife. As we noted in Chapter 3, married women are now often in paid employment and they, rather than men, are taking up many of the new jobs in the service sector. However, they do so more frequently on a part-time, low-paid basis and, because of the limited hours, they are not insured in their own right. (In addition, the number of one-person households has increased from 17% in 1971 to 24% in 1985 and it seems as if this trend will continue.)

Welfare will also need to distinguish between work, and employment as only one form of work. It will need to encourage all forms of work – voluntary, co-operative and self-provision-ing, as well as that which is employment-based.[33] It will need to allow people to be creative in their choice of options and how they combine one option with another.

These aims require, as previously, different levels of welfare – preventive, developmental and remedial – and the latter will need to take account of casualties of a changing economy who, in a more stable period, would not have been in trouble and would have continued to manage their own affairs and exercise their own autonomy. Just as in the Industrial Revolution, the workings of the market are actually preventing the well-being of a large number of people. Welfare also needs to recognise that people develop and change at different rates. Slower changers may make the more substantial change in the long run, but should not need to become casualties in the process.

If the 'welfare state' has an aura of complacent philanthropy to the indigent and delinquent, it could, as suggested by Trist, become a 'service state', committed to the well-being and development of all its citizens. A service state would need to take account of the level of the hierarchy of need to which people have become accustomed and not carelessly plunge the casualties of social change back to a bare survival level as at present. It would need to regard the importance for the individual of finding a meaning for living when employment will not, as in the past, be one of the main keystones of life for a sizeable minority. Even more difficult, it will need to attempt to heal the social split and find a redefinition of creative use of time for those not in employment and which is recognised as valid by the employed majority. It cannot afford any further 'slumming-up' of previously robust industrial towns, suburbs and over-spill estates and become a ghetto-type society in which pockets of the population are characterised by their frustration and apathy. It cannot afford the inevitable violence that will ensue.

As Gosling has said,

It is certainly no use defining a large minority in terms of a negative.

I am thunderstruck by the fact that in all likelihood about one in five of the population will live their lives without the benefit or the curse of employment, without earning their living in the old fashioned sense. In the past this minority has been smaller and has been treated to a fair amount of split moral projection: reverential if rich, and abusive if poor – gypsies, bums, layabouts, the unemployable, etc. If the latter is now to become a distinct way of life within a society that still holds (at least for some time to come) to the group norms of productivity, service, remuneration, etc., then some means of negotiating across the boundary between these two sub-groups needs to be developed and some redeployment of mutual projections effected. Might the 'unemployed' of the post-industrial society become, for example, the repository of society's more reflective and contemplative values, its priesthood?[34]

These ideas have immense implications for education. In the past, education, training, work and retirement have followed each other in orderly succession. Increasingly, learning, working and relaxing will need to be in closer juxtaposition. As a large number of unskilled and semi-skilled jobs become automated and computerised, the jobs that remain will involve mainly perceptual, conceptual and interpersonal skills. Qualification to enter this world of employment will be raised to a higher level.

As what are now new technologies get outdated by even newer ones, there will need to be a constant re-learning and re-training. In order to work creatively at this higher level, people will need 're-creative' experiences as well as relaxation.

Leisure (time at one's own disposal), which obtains meaning only by contrast to the effort of work, will need to be re-defined for those whose leisure derives from their unemployment. Finally a service state needs to take account of man's 'social unsociability' and his resistance to change. In the process of change from industrialism to post-industrialism, welfare will need to sustain and contain people to enable them to grapple with the changes and to find their own continuity, whereby the reality of the new can be related to the reality of the old. The provision of basic services and developmental opportunities needs support from counselling services not just for the redundant and not just focussed on re-start of employment. These services need to allow space for grief for a way of life which has been lost before a creative adaptation can be made to a new way of life. Such services can only be provided and maintained in a society which recognises that this grief is natural, necessary and, if allowed, eventually developmental.

It is not surprising, therefore, that in the present social climate a plethora of *private* counselling and therapy services have sprung into existence. When social roles are no longer prescribed by tradition, when options proliferate, when social and psychological values are changing, when the development of the individual is generally espoused, then those who can afford the fees use counselling or therapy to help them sort out their own uniqueness: who they are and who they want to be, and what is in their capacity if they are emotionally free enough from internal constraints to adapt and explore new avenues open to them.

One of the present sadnesses is that individual and family counselling, or casework, as it used to be called, has over recent years taken a back seat in the complex role which the modern social worker employed by the state has to handle. Quite properly much emphasis has been put on community work, which is vital in a period of social turbulence. It is a live and lively community which can be the main container during a process of change when groups of people are needing to adapt and in doing so needing to relate the new to the old. Yet on its own it is not enough. Within any community are many individuals more constrained by *internal* than external pressures – the old ghosts, demons and symbols we described in earlier chapters of this book. Their problems have their own uniqueness and unless attended to on a unique basis will continue to incapacitate them. Our *ideal* service state will need to provide for uniqueness as well as to offer firm containment for those who cannot afford the private services.

This book ends with no neat conclusions. We remind the reader that it is a book of ideas – 'rudimentary ideas'. In this final chapter we have argued for a less defensive attitude to welfare. We believe that in the long run the existing attitude will lead to further fragmentation of society, continue to sap energy and reduce the adaptive capability which is so urgently required in the present social and economic climate. We have promoted a more active concept of welfare which certainly needs to reduce the ill-fare and social injustice that our clients and other groups of disadvantaged people experience, but also to recognise that needs have developed in our society beyond survival ones. We have human faculties to satisfy them if we choose. The best welfare is that which promotes and enhances people's potential intellectual and emotional development. In doing so, it in no way saps resources. It adds to them.

We consider this to be a valid aim accompanied by a spark of hope – an image of what the future could be. Action without ideas and hope leaves all effort 'meaningless, drab, grey and profoundly miserable'. Hope does not exclude awareness of the struggle that will be needed to achieve some of these aims, nor the problems or conflict which are engendered in any process of change. Change requires flexible institutions, and institutions we know are slow to change. The 'unsocial sociability' of man – our greed, our self-centredness, our envy – may well preclude such change.

The idea of the type of service state we and others have suggested inevitably provokes conflict as different groups fight to maintain their previously achieved position without enough regard for other less fortunate groups. Can we enter the conflict? Can we struggle for meaning in our personal, professional and political life knowing that future life is now structured by an apparently ever increasing interdependence throughout the world? Can we respect the inevitable tension between the promotion of individual autonomy and the need for us all to become more sociable social creatures?

Appendix I
The Samples

I. Description of families

1. Social Class*

		Clinical sample	Workshop sample	Total
Class	I	4	1	5
	II	15	7	22
	III N	2	6	8
	III M	3	9	12
	IV	1	3	4
	V	0	6	6
	Unknown	0	2	2
	Total	25	34	59

* As defined by husband's Occupation Code published by OPCCS. HMSO 1980

2. Age of unemployed partner

		Clinical sample		Workshop sample		Total	
		Husband	Wife	Husband	Wife	Husband	Wife
Under 25		–	–	2	–	2	–
	25-35	6	–	14	–	21	
	36-50	15	1	8	2	23	3
Over	51-60	4	–	8	–	12	
Unknown		–	–	1	–	1	
Total		25	1	33	2	58+	3+

† Both members of one couple in the clinical sample and one couple in the
workshop sample were unemployed.

196

3. Number of children per family

No. of children in family	Clinical sample families	Workshop sample families	Total
0	6	2	8
1	5	3	8
2	11	18	29
3	2	6	8
4	1	3	4
5	0	2	2
Total	25	34	59

4. Number of children under 18 years

No. of children in family	Clinical sample families	Workshop sample families	Total
1	5	4	9
2	8	15	23
3	2	3	5
4	0	3	3
5	0	1	1
Total	15	26	41

II. Employment/unemployment

1. Length of unemployment
(at the time of first seeking help)

Unemployment	Clinical sample		Workshop sample		Total	
	Husband	Wife	Husband	Wife	Husband	Wife
pending	2	1	0	–	2	1
Less than 6 months	2	–	3	–	5	–
1-2 years	14	–	14	–	28	–
2-3 years	1	–	3	–	4	–
Over 4	1	–	2	1	3	1
Unknown	–	–	3	–	3	–
Total	24	1	33	1	57	2

2. Lost occupations

Clinical sample		Workshop sample	
Husband	Wife	Husband	Wife
Advertising Executive		Apron Manager	
Airline Pilot		Army Instructor	
2 Architects		Artist (graphic)	
Company Executive		Bank Manager	
Computer Programmer		Civil Servant (Clerk)	
Despatch Rider		Clerk	
2 Journalists		Electrician	
Merchant Navy Officer		Engineer (Merchant Navy)	
2 Musicians		2 Farm Labourers	
Painter		Glass Cutter	
Printer		Handyman	
Public Affairs Manager		Linguist	Linguist
Roofer		5 Labourers	
Service Engineer	Shop Proprietor	Lorry Driver	
Social Worker		Office Manager	
2 Solicitors		2 Mechanics	
Store Clerk		Phototechnician	
2 Teachers		2 Policemen	
Theatre Director		Police Warder	
Wine Trade Clerk		Rep. (Chemical Co.)	
		Salesman	
		Shipyard Worker	
		Storekeeper	
		Technologist	Teacher

3. Employment of both partners
(before loss of employment of one partner or both)

Employment	Clinical sample		Workshop sample		Total	
	Husband	Wife	Husband	Wife	Husband	Wife
Full time paid	21	14	29	5	49	19
Part time paid	–	6	–	3	–	9
Irregular paid	4	–	4	1	8	1
Housewife/husband	–	5	–	24	–	29
Unknown	–	–	2	1	2	1

4. Occupations of paid employed partners

Clinical sample		Workshop sample	
Husband	Wife	Husband	Wife
	Media technician	Headmaster	Artist (graphic)
	2 Antique Dealers		2 Bank Clerks
	Computer Programme		Barmaid
	Dancer		Nurse
	Fine Arts Journalist		Saleswoman/
	2 Managers		Receptionist
	Medical Practitioner		Secretary
	Nurse		Teacher
	Probation Officer		Waitress
	Psychologist		
	2 Secretaries		
	Social Worker		
	Solicitor		
	Speech Therapist		
	Teacher		

Appendix II

Advertised Description of Workshop

The aim of this workshop is to provide an opportunity for practitioners currently working with marriages and families affected by unemployment

    i)   to share and develop understanding of the psychological effects which job loss has on marital and family relationships

    ii)   to explore professional difficulties inherent in working with these problems

Structure

The workshop will consist of three parts:

Part I   24th – 28th September 1984   at the University of Exeter
9.30 a.m. to 5.00 p.m.
non residential

Part II   29th September 1984 to 1st January 1985   in participants' own Service

Part III   2nd – 5th January 1985   at the University of Exeter
9.30 a.m. – 5.00 p.m.
non residential

Part I will provide opportunities for exploration of ideas derived from the literature on the subject and from case material presented by workshop leaders and by members.

Part II will provide members with an opportunity to test out and apply ideas presented in Part I as appropriate in their own work setting.

Part III will provide an opportunity for these ideas to be re-examined in the light of the experience gained in Part II and for hypotheses to be refined.

Parts I and III will be structured into three types of events:

i) lectures and discussions in plenary sessions. Institute leaders will offer a theoretical framework developed from their own clinical work with couples affected by unemployment

ii) work discussion groups in which participants will present detailed material from their own experience with couples affected by unemployment with whom they are currently working. These groups will examine:

    a) the nature of and changes in the interaction between the couple with particular reference to

    b) the nature of the anxiety aroused by unemployment and the effect of this anxiety on the couple and on the worker (particularly if that worker's job is, or could be, under threat);

iii) plenary sessions in which members will review their experience and evaluate the workshop

Leadership

The workshop will be led by four staff members of the Institute of Marital Studies

Janet Mattinson
Diana Daniell
Nina Cohen
Stan Ruszczynski

and four senior officers of the Devon services

Membership

Membership is by invitation, and is open to qualified and experienced workers undertaking pastoral counselling, probation and prison aftercare, general social work, marriage guidance counselling, medical practice, health visiting, education welfare and counselling.

Members will need to commit themselves to all three parts of the workshop and to present their own case material. They need to understand that this workshop is part of a wider research programme, and they will be joining the workshop leaders in the capacity of fellow research-workers. Within this context, the workshop will be recorded and some of the material eventually used in a publication. (No material will be used in this way without discussion with and permission of the particular member who will be able to comment on the draft and changes of otherwise identifying facts.)

Those people wishing to be invited to join this workshop should do so through their department, agency or organisation with a covering statement about their professional background, experience with unemployed clients or patients and reasons for wanting to participate.

Appendix III

Members of Workshops

London

Group leaders

Miss D Daniell
Mr S Ruszczynski

Devon

Group leaders

Mr C Buttle
Mrs N Cohen
Miss D Daniell
Revd A Lovewell
Miss J Mattinson
Mr S Ruszczynski

Tyneside

Group leaders

Miss J Birkby
Miss D Daniell
Mrs B Hester
Revd J Lowen
Miss J Mattinson
Mr S Ruszczynski

Members

Ms C Davies
Mr N Hunt
Mrs R Klauber
Ms V McKennell
Mrs B Mackenzie
Mr R McNeill
Mr T Prendergast
Ms P Zeff

Members

Mrs H Berry
Mrs L Culverhouse
Mrs C Cousins
Mr H Dayes
Mrs J Dixon
Mrs D Durban
*Mr D Duffus
Mrs C Facey
*Mrs G Feest
*Mr C Ford
Mrs J Green
Mrs H Heatley
Mrs S Hutchins
Mrs A Jordan
Mrs J Langworthy
Revd J Laverack
Mrs P Lettington
Mr P Millett
Mrs S Mumford
Miss E Northey
*Mrs V Parfrey
*Ms P Paterson
Mrs J Sinden
Ms C Vincent
Mr M Waldron
Mrs G Widdows

Members

Mrs L Birtwistle
Revd R Burston
Revd S Connelly
Revd F Dexter
Revd G Earney
Mrs J Endean
Mrs S Frater
Mrs A Hall
Ms E Kelly
Revd P Kenny
Mr B Langley
Mrs D Marshall
Mrs C Spungin
Revd N Taylor
Mrs S Townsin
Mrs A Walton
Mrs S Winters

* Attended only Part I

References

Introduction

1. Ramprakash, D. (ed.) 1985. *Social Trends* 15. London, HMSO.
2. Murch, M. 1979. Evidence to Government Working Party, quoted in *Marriage Matters*. London, HMSO. Chester, R. 1971. 'Health and Marriage Breakdown. Experience of a Sample of Divorced Women'. *Brit. J. Prev. & Soc. Med. 25*
3. Pugh, G. & Cohen, N. 1984. 'Presentation of Marital Problems in General Practice'. *The Practitioner*, July, vol. 228
4. Smith, R. 1985. 'Occupational Health'. *Brit. Med. J.* 7 Dec. vol. 29. College, M. & Bartholomew, R. 1980. *A Study on the Long Term Unemployed*. London, Manpower Services Commission. Linn, M.W. *et al.* 1985. 'Effects of Unemployment on Mental & Physical Health'. *Am. J. Public Health* 75
5. Platt, S. 1984. 'Unemployment & Suicidal Behaviour: A Review of the Literature'. *Soc. Sc. & Med.* 19 (2)
6. Ramprakash, D. (ed.) 1985. op. cit.
7. Daniell, D. 1985. 'Love and Work: Complementary Aspects of Personal Identity.' *Int. J. Soc. Ec.* 12, no. 2.

1. Purpose and Meaning

1. Maslow, A.H., 1954. *Motivation and Personality*. London, Harper & Row.
2. Erikson, E.H. 1959. 'Identity and the Life Cycle. Selected Papers'. *Psych. Issues*, I no.1. N.Y. Int. Univ. Press, Inc.
3. Strauss, A.L. 1969. *Mirrors and Masks: The Search for Identity*. Martin Robertson (now Oxford, Blackwell)
4. Hartman, H. 1958. *Ego Psychology and the Problem of Adaptation*. N.Y. Int. Univ. Press, Inc.
5. Erikson, E.H. 1950. op. cit.
6. For example: Bernstein, B. 1961. 'Social Class and Linguistic Development: A Theory of Social Learning'. In Halsey, A.H. *et al. Education Economy and Society*. Toronto, Collier-Macmillan. Brown, G. 1982. 'Early Loss and Depression'. In Parkes, C.M. and Stevenson-Hinde, J. (ed.) *The Place of Attachment in Human Behaviour*. London, Tavistock. Biller, H.B. 1971. *Father, Child and Sex Role: Paternal Determination of Personality Development*. Heath, Lexington.
7. For example: Freud, S. 1949. 'An Outline of Psycho-Analysis'. *S.E.* XXIII. London, Hogarth Press. Klein, M. 1975. 'Our Adult World and Its Roots in Infancy'. In *Envy and Gratitude and Other Works, 1946-1963*. London, Hogarth Press. Winnicott, D.W. 1972. 'Ego Distortion in Terms of True and False Self'. In *The Maturational Process and the Facilitating Environment*. London, Hogarth Press. Jung, C.G. 1934. 'The Development of Personality'. *Collected Works*, vol. 17. London, Routledge & Kegan Paul.

8. Curtis, R. 1986. 'Household and Family in Theory of Inequality'. *Am. Sociol. Rev.* 51.
9. Erikson, E.H. 1959. (quoting a saying of Freud). op. cit.
10. Anthony, P.D. 1977. *Ideology of Work*. London, Lawrence & Wishart.

2. Making a Living

1. Marx, K. and Engels, F. 1970. Arthur, C.J. (ed.) *The German Ideology*. London, Lawrence & Wishart.
2. Pope John Paul II. 1981. *Laborem Exercens*. Third Encyclical.
3. Anthony, P.D. 1977. *Ideology of Work*. London, Lawrence & Wishart.
4. Sabine, G.H. 1951. *The Works of Gerard Winstanley*. Ithaca, Cornell University.
5. Anthony, P.D. 1977. op. cit.
6. Zimmern, A.W. 1915. *The Greek Commonwealth*. Oxford, University Press.
7. ibid.
8. Pahl, R.E. 1984. *Divisions of Labour*. Oxford, Basil Blackwell.
9. Stenton, D. 1978. *The English Woman in History*. N.Y., Shocken Books
10. Anthony, P.D. 1977. op cit.
11. Ramprakash, D. (ed.) 1985. *Social Trends* 15. London, HMSO.
12. Pahl, R.E. 1984. op cit.
13. Burnett, J. 1974. *Useful Toil*. London, Allen Lane.
14. ibid.
15. Sarason, S.B. 1977. *Work, Ageing and Social Change*. N.Y., Free Press.
16. Cherniss, C. 1980. *Staff Burnout: Job Stress in the Human Services*. London, Sage.
17. ibid.
18. Institute of Personnel Management. 1973. Memorandum.
19. Marx, K. 1964. *Early Writings*. Harmondsworth, Penguin.
20. Pahl, R.E. 1984. op. cit.
21. ibid.
22. Burnett, J. 1974. op. cit.
23. Cooper, C.L. and Marshall, J. 1978. *Understanding Executive Stress*. London, Macmillan.
24. Terkel, S. 1974. *Working*. Harmondsworth, Penguin.
25. Cooper, C.L. and Marshall, J. 1978. op. cit.
26. Kearns, J. 1986. Quoted by Sherman, J. 'Illness Caused by Stress at Work'. *The Times*. London.
27. Freudenberger, H.J. 1983. 'Burnout: Contemporary Issues, Trends and Concerns'. In Farber, B.A. *Introduction to Stress and Burnout in the Human Service Professions*. Oxford, Pergamon Press.
28. Cherniss, C. 1980. op. cit.
29. Terkel, S. 1974. op. cit.
30. Barter, J. 1978. *Computers and Employment*. London, National Opinion Polls Ltd.
31. Morse, N.C. and Weiss, R.S. 1955. 'The Function and Meaning of Work and the Job'. *Am. Sociol. Rev.* 20.
32. Heller, F. In press. *The Meaning of Working*.
33. Morse, N.C. and Weiss, R.S. 1955. op. cit.
34. Jahoda, M, 1979. 'The Impact of Unemployment in the 1930s and the

1970s'. *Bull. Brit. Psychol. Soc.* 32.

35. Willis, P.E. 1976. 'Human Experience and Material Production: The Culture of the Shop Floor'. *Working Papers in Cultural Studies* 9. Spring.

36. Menninger, K.A. 1942. 'Work as a Sublimation'. *Bull. of the Menninger Clinic.* 6.

37. Quoted by Taylor, W.S. 1933. 'A Critique of Sublimation in Males'. *Gen. Psychol. Mono.* 13.

38. Menninger, K.A. op. cit.

39. Moss Kanter, R. 1984. *The Change Masters: Corporate Entrepreneurs at Work.* London, Allen & Unwin.

40. Yassukovitch, S. Quoted by Appleyard, B. 1986. 'Running Scared and Fast'. *The Times.* London.

41. Carlyle, T. 1843. *Past and Present. Book III.* (ed.) Altick, R.D. 1977. New York, University Press.

42. For example: Valient, G.E. *et al.* 1972. 'Some Psychologic Vulnerabilities of Physicians'. *New Eng. J. Med.* Menninger, K.A. 1957. 'Psychological Factors in the Choice of Medicine as a Profession'. *Bull. of the Menninger Clinic* 21.

43. Rarcusir, G.R. *et al.* 1981. 'Becoming a Therapist: Dynamics and Career Choice'. *Prof. Psychol.* 12, no 2.

44. Skynner, R. 1964. 'Group Analytic Themes in Training and Case Discussion Groups'. *6th Int. Confer. Psychother. Selected Lectures.*

45. Abse, L. 1973. *Private Member.* London, Macdonald.

46. Evans, C. *Living Language.* In draft.

47. Pruyser, P.W. 1980. 'Work: Curse or Blessing'. *Bull. of the Menninger Clinic.* 44.

48. Terkel, S. op. cit.

49. Menzies, I.E.P. 1960. 'A Case Study in Functioning of Social Systems as a Defence Against Anxiety: A Report on a Study of the Nursing Service in a General Hospital'. *Human Relations 13*, no: 2.

50. Lawrence, W.G. 1982. 'Some Psychic and Political Dimensions of Work Experiences'. *Occasional Papers* 2. London, Tavistock Institute of Human Relations.

51. James, B. 1986, 'A Force to be Reasoned with'. *The Times.* London.

3. Making a Loving

1. Fox, R. 1975. *Encounter with Anthropology.* London, Peregrine.

2. Bowlby, J. 1969. *Attachment and Loss*, vol. 1. London, Hogarth Press & Institute of Psychoanalysis.

3. Mattinson, J. & Sinclair, I. 1979. *Mate and Stalemate.* Oxford, Blackwell.

4. Mansfield, P. 1985. *Young People and Marriage.* Edinburgh, Scottish Marriage Guidance Council.

5. Leach, E.R. 1972. In Pole, N. (ed.) *Environmental Solutions.* Cambridge.

6. Macfarlane, A. 1978. *The Origins of English Individualism.* Oxford, Blackwell.

7. Houlbrooke, R.A. 1984. *The English Family 1450 – 1700.* Harlow, Longman.

8. Macfarlane, A. 1978. op. cit.

9. Bernard, J. 1982. *The Future of Marriage.* Harmondsworth, Penguin.

10. Houlbrooke, R.A. 1982. op. cit.

11. ibid.

12. Sarsby, J. 1983. *Romantic Love and Society.* Harmondsworth, Penguin.

13. Thompson, E. 1976 *Social Trends.* London, HMSO.

14. Madge, J. & Brown, C. 1981. *First Homes: A Survey of the Housing Circumstances of Young Married Couples*. London, Policy Studies Institute.
15. Houlbrooke, R.A. op. cit.
16. Griffin, T. (Ed.) 1987. *Social Trends* 17. London, HMSO.
17. Halsey, A.H. 1987. 'Social Trends Since World War II'. In Griffin, T. (Ed.) op. cit.
18. Mount, F. 1982. *The Subversive Family*. London, Cape.
19. ibid.
20. Ephesians 5:22
21. Houlbrooke, R.A. 1982. op. cit.
22. ibid.
23. Forster, M. 1984. *Significant Sisters*. Harmondsworth, Penguin.
24. Griffin, T. (ed.) 1987. op. cit.
25. ibid.
26. ibid.
27. Gorer, G. 1971. *Sex and Marriage in England Today*. London, Nelson.
28. Halsey, A.H. 1987. op. cit.
29. Mansfield, P. 1982. 'A Portrait of Contemporary Marriage: Equal Partners or Just Good Companions'. In Guy, C. (compiler). *Change in Marriage*. Rugby, NNGC.
30. Halsey, A.H. 1987. op. cit.
31. Griffin, T. 1987. op. cit.
32. Finch, J. 1985. 'Work, the Family and the Home: A more Egalitarian Future? *Int. J. Soc. Ec.* 12. no. 2.
33. Mansfield, P. 1982. op. cit.
34. Ramprakash, D. (ed.) 1985. *Social Trends* 15. London, HMSO.
35. ibid.
36. Allatt, P. & Yeandle, S.M. 1985. *Family Structure and Youth Unemployment in an Area of Persistent Decline*. Unpublished Report. University of Durham.
37. Mount, F. 1982. op. cit.
38. Houlbrooke, R.A. 1984. op. cit.
39. Gough, R. 1834. *The History of Myddle*. Harmondsworth, Penguin (1981).
40. Houlbrooke, R.A. 1984 op. cit.
41. Emmanuel, le R.D. 1978. *Montaillou*. Harmondsworth, Penguin.
42. Colman, M. 1982. *Continuous Excursions*. London, Pluto Press.
43. Houlbrooke, R.A. 1984. op. cit.
44. Quoted by Houlbrooke, R.A. 1984. op. cit.
45. Davis, N. (ed.) 1983. *The Paston Letters*. Oxford, University Press.
46. Macfarlane, A. 1970. *The Family Life of Ralph Josselin, A Seventeenth Century Clergyman: An Essay in Historical Anthropology*. Cambridge, University Press.
47. Pincus, L. (ed.) 1960. *Marriage: Emotional Conflict and Growth*. London, Institute of Marital Studies.
48. Stevens, A. 1982. *Archetype: A Natural History of the Self*. London, Routledge and Kegan Paul.
49. Bowlby, J. 1979. *The Making and Breaking of Affectional Bonds*. London, Tavistock.
50. Bernard, J. 1976. op. cit.
51. Segal, J. 1985. *Phantasy in Everyday Life*. Harmondsworth, Penguin.
52. Huxley, A. 1955. *The Genius and the Goddess*. London, Triad/Panther.
53. Freud, S. 1922. 'Group Psychology and the Analysis of the Ego'. *S.E.*

XVIII. London, Hogarth Press.
54. Byng-Hall, S. 1985. 'Resolving Distance Conflicts'. In Gurman, A.S. *Casebook of Marital Therapy*. London, The Guilford Press.
55. de Riencourt, A. 1983. *Woman and Power in History*. London, Honeyglen Publishing.
56. Hennig, M. & Jardin, A. 1977. *The Managerial Woman*. N.Y., Anchor Press/Doubleday.
57. Clark, D. *et al*. 1985. 'Work and Marriage in the Offshore Oil Industry'. *Int. J. Soc. Ec.* 12, no. 2.
58. Davidson, M. & Cooper, C. 1985. 'Women Managers: Work, Stress and Marriage'. *Int. J. Soc. Ec.* 12, no. 2.
59. G.M.B. 1987. *Winning a Fair Deal for Women*. Esher, General Municipal Boilermakers and Allied Trades Union.
60. ibid.
61. Knight, L. 1986. 'Married to Affairs of State'. *The Times*. 5 November. London.
62. ibid.
63. Finch, J. 1983. *Married to the Job: Wives' Incorporation in Men's Work*. London, Allen & Unwin.
64. ibid.

4. Signals

1. Mattinson, J. & Sinclair, I. 1979. *Mate and Stalemate*. Oxford, Basil Blackwell and 1980, London, Institute of Marital Studies.
2. Murch, M. 1979. Evidence to Government Working Party quoted in *Marriage Matters*. London, HMSO. Chester, R. 1971. 'Health and Marriage Breakdown Experience of a Sample of Divorced Women'. *Brit. J. Prev. & Soc. Med.* 25
3. Pugh, G. & Cohen, N. 1984. 'Presentation of Marital Problems in General Practice'. *The Practitioner* 228, July.
4. Higgs, R. 1984. 'Life Changes'. *Br. Med. J.* 288
5. Beale, N. & Nethercott, S. 1985. 'Job Loss and Family Morbidity: a study of a factory closure'. *J. Roy. Coll. Gen. Practit.* 35, November.

5. 'Oh Absalom'

1. Peretz, D. 1970. 'Reaction to Loss'. In Schoenberg, B. *et al.* (eds.) *Loss and Grief: Psychological Management in Medical Practice*. N.Y., Columbia Univ. Press.
2. Marris, P. 1974. *Loss and Change*. London, Routledge & Kegan Paul.
3. Freud, S. 1917. 'Mourning and Melancholia'. *S.E.* 14. London, Hogarth Press.
4. Darwin, C. 1859. *The Origin of Species by Means of Natural Selection*. London, Murray.
5. Lindmann, E. 1944. 'Symptomatology and Management of Acute Grief'. *Am. J. Psych.* 101. Marris, P. 1974 op. cit. Parkes, C.M. 1969. 'Separation Anxiety: An Aspect of the Search for a Lost Object'. In Lader, H.M. *Studies of Anxiety*. London, Headley. Parkes, C.M. 1971. 'The First Year of Bereavement: A Longitudinal Study of the Reactions of London Widows to the Death of their Husbands'. *Psych.* 33
6. Bowlby, J. 1979. 'Separation and Loss Within the Family'. In *The Making*

and Breaking of Affectional Bonds. London, Tavistock.
7. Parkes, C.M. 1969. op. cit.
8. Lewis, C.S. 1966. *A Grief Observed*. London, Faber & Faber.
9. Bowlby, J. 1970. op. cit.
10. Maddison, D. & Walker, W.L. 1967. 'Factors Affecting the Outcome of Conjugal Bereavement'. *Brit. J. Psych.* 113
11. Lewis, C.S. 1966. op. cit.
12. Deutsche, H. 1938. 'Absence of Grief'. *Psychoanal. Qu.* 6
13. Parkes, C.M. 1972. 'Components of the Reactions to Loss of a Limb, Spouse or Home'. *J. Psychosom. Res.* 16
14. ibid.
15. Marris, P. 1974. op. cit.
16. Erikson, E. 1979. 'Identity and the Life Cycle : Selected Papers'. *Psychol. Issues* 1.
17. Marris, P. 1974. op. cit.
18. Beales, H.L. & Lambert, R.S. (eds.) 1934. *Memoirs of the Unemployed*, 1973. Wakefield, E.P. Publishing. Eisenberg, P. & Lazarsfield, P. 1938. 'The Psychological Effects of Unemployment'. *Psychol. Bull.* 35. Orwell, G. 1927. *The Road to Wigan Pier*. 1962. Harmondsworth, Penguin. Jahoda, M. *et al.* 1933. *Marienthal – The Sociography of an Unemployed Community*. 1972. London, Tavistock. Bakke, E.W. 1933. *The Unemployed Man*. London, Nisbet.
19. Hill, J. 1978. 'The Social and Psychological Impact of Unemployment'. *New Society* 19 Jan. Fagin, L. & Little, M. 1984. *The Forsaken Families*. Harmondsworth, Penguin. Kelvin, P. & Jarrett, J. 1985. *Unemployment: Its Psychological Effects*. Cambridge, C.U.P.
20. Fagin, L. & Little, M. 1984. ibid.
21. Hill, J., 1978. op. cit.
22. ibid.
23. ibid.
24. ibid.
25. Ramprakash, D. (ed.) 1985. *Social Trends* 15. London, HMSO.
26. Haskey, J. 1986. 'Grounds for Divorce in England and Wales – A Social and Demographic Analysis'. *J. Biosoc. Sci.* 18.
27. Beale, N. & Nethercote, S. 1985. 'Job Loss and Family Morbidity: A Study of a Factory Closure. *J. Roy. Coll. Gen. Practs.* 35
28. Platt, S.D. 1984. 'Unemployment and Suicidal Behaviour: A Review of the Literature'. *Soc. Sc. Med.* 19.
29. Platt, S. & Kreitman, N. 1984. 'Trends in Parasuicide and Unemployment among Men in Edinburgh, 1968-82'. *Brit. Med J.* 289.
30. See 18 & 19 above.
31. Klein, M. 1937. 'Love, Guilt and Reparation'. In *Love, Guilt and Reparation and other Works*. 1981. London, Hogarth Press.
32. Marris, P. 1974. op. cit.
33. Bernard, J. 1976. *The Future of Marriage*. Harmondsworth, Penguin.
34. Deutsche, H. 1937. op. cit.
35. Seabrook, J. 1983. Unemployment. St. Albans, Granada.
36. Miller, S. 1985. *The Shame Experience*. London, The Analytic Press.
37. Archbishop of Canterbury's Commission. 1985. *Faith in the City*. London, Church House.
38. Seabrook, J. 1983. op. cit.
39. Illich, I. 1978. *The Right to Useful Employment*. London, Marion Boyars.
40. Canterbury. 1985. op. cit.

41. Jahoda, M. *et al.* 1933. op. cit.
42. Canterbury. 1985. op. cit.
43. Donnison, D. In Canterbury. 1985. op. cit.
44. Canterbury. 1985. op. cit.
45. ibid.
46. ibid.
47. ibid.
48. Seabrook, J. 1983. op. cit.
49. Canterbury. 1985. op. cit.
50. ibid.
51. Hill, J. 1977. op. cit.
52. Kelvin, P. & Jarrett, J. 1985. op. cit.
53. Flaim, P. 1973. 'Discouraged Workers and Changes in Employment'. *Monthly Labour Rev.* 96 (13).
54. Kelvin, P. & Jarrett, J. 1983. op. cit.
55. ibid.
56. Canterbury, 1985. op. cit.
57. Freeman, H.L. 1984. 'The Scientific Background'. In *Mental Health and the Environment*. London, Churchill Livingstone.
58. Freeman, H.L. 1984. op. cit.
59. ibid.
60. Kelvin, P. & Jarrett, J. 1958. op. cit.

6. Reverberations

1. Lidz, T. 1946. 'Nightmares and the Combat Neuroses'. *Psychiat.* 9.
2. Hartman, E. 1984. *The Nightmare: The Psychology and Biology of Terrifying Dreams*. N.Y., Basic Books.

7. Daylight Robbery

1. Atchley, R.C. 1976. *The Sociology of Retirement*. Cambridge, Massachusetts, Schenkman.
2. Dunn, D. 1985. 'Getting Used to It'. In *Secret Villages*. London, Faber & Faber.
3. Byng-Hall, J. 1985. 'Resolving Distance Conflicts'. In Gurman, A.S. (ed.) *Casebook of Marital Therapy*. London, Guilford Press.
4. Crabb, G. 1816. *Crabb's English Synonyms*. 1979. London, Routledge & Kegan Paul.
5. Klein, M. 1957. 'Envy and Gratitude'. In 1975 *Envy and Gratitude and Other Works 1946-1963*. London, Hogarth Press.

8. Under the Influence

1. Freud, S. 1915. 'The Unconscious'. *S.E.* XIV. London, The Hogarth Press.
2. Greenson, R. 1967. *The Technique and Practice of Psychoanalysis*, vol. I. London, The Hogarth Press.
3. Joseph, B. 1985. 'Transference: The Total Situation'. *Int. J. Psycho-Anal.* 66.
4. Jung, C.G. 1935. Lecture V in *Analytical Psychology: Its Theory and Practice*. London, Routledge and Kegan Paul.
5. Searles, H.F. 1955. 'The Informational Value of the Supervisor's Emotional

Experience'. In *Collected Papers on Schizophrenia and Related Subjects*. London, The Hogarth Press. Mattinson, J. 1975. *The Reflection Process in Casework Supervision*. London, The Institute of Marital Studies.
6. Searles, H.F. 1955. op. cit.
7. Segal, H. 1975. *Introduction to the Works of Melanie Klein*. London, The Hogarth Press.
8. Klein, M. 1957. 'Envy and Gratitude'. In 1975 *Envy and Gratitude and other Works 1946-1963*. London, The Hogarth Press.
9. Klein, M. 1956. 'Envy and Gratitude'. In Mitchell, J. (ed). 1986 *The Selected Melanie Klein*. Harmondsworth, Penguin Books.
10. Jung, C.J. 1946. 'The Psychology of the Transference'. *Coll. Works 1954*, vol. 16. London, Routledge & Kegan Paul.

9. The Management of Change

1. Titmus, R. 1954. 'The Administrative Setting of Social Services'. *Case Conference* 1, no. 1.
2. Parkes, C. 1984. Foreword in Fagin, L. & Little, M. *The Forsaken Families*. Harmondsworth, Penguin.
3. The *Independent*. 1987. London. 28 May.
4. ibid.
5. Rajan, A. & Pearson, R. 1986. *United Kingdom Occupation and Employment Trends to 1990*. London, Butterworth.
6. National Institute of Economic & Social Research 1987. *Nat. Inst. Ec. Rev.* 120, May.
7. Riesman, D. 1958. 'Leisure and Work in Post-Industrial Society'. In Larraby, E. & Mayershon, R. (eds). *Mass Leisure*. Glencoe, Ill. Free Press.
8. Emery, F. & Trist, E. 1972. *Towards A Social Ecology*. London, Plenum Press.
9. ibid.
10. Toffler, A. 1970. *Future Shock*. N.Y., Random House.
11. Sutherland, J. 1974. *The Psychodynamic Image of Man*. Aberdeen, Univ. Press.
12. Heller, F. In press. *The Meaning of Working*. London, Academic Press.
13. Emery, F. & Trist, E. 1972. op. cit.
14. ibid.
15. Freud, S. 1913. 'The Claims of Psychoanalysis to Scientific Interest'. *S.E.* 13.
16. Jung, C. 1935. 'The Relations between the Ego and the Unconscious'. *Coll. Works* 7. London, Routledge & Kegan Paul.
17. Jacques, E. 1955. 'Social Systems as a Defence against Persecutory and Depressive Anxiety'. In Klein, M. *New Directions in Psychoanalysis*. London, Tavistock. Menzies, I. 1960. 'A Case Study in Functioning of Social Systems as a Defence against Anxiety: A Report on a Study of the Nursing System of a General Hospital'. *Human Relations* 13, no. 2. May.
18. Marris, P. 1974. *Loss and Change*. London, Routledge & Kegan Paul.
19. Laurance, J. 1986. 'Unemployment: Health Hazards'. *New Soc.* 21 March.
20. Smith, R. 1985. 'Occupationless Health'. *Brit. Med. J.* 291. 14 December.
21. Laurance, J. 1986. op. cit.
22. Veitch, A. 1986. *Guardian*. London, 5 July.
23. Fowles, J. 1977. *Daniel Martin*. London, Cape.
24. *The Times*. 1987. 'Emotions at the Pithead'. 21 July.

25. Dahrendorf, R. 1979. *Life Chances*. London, Weidenfeld & Nicolson.
26. Jordan, B. 1985. *The State: Authority and Autonomy*. Oxford, Blackwell.
27. ibid.
28. ibid.
29. Emery, F. & Trist, E. 1972. op. cit.
30. Kant, I. 'Idea Towards a General History with Cosmopolitan Intent. Fourth Proposition'. Translated by Dahrendorf, R. 1979. op. cit.
31. Emery, F. & Trist, E. 1972. op. cit.
32. Jordan, B. 1987. *Rethinking Welfare*. Oxford, Blackwell.
33. ibid.
34. Gosling, R. 1983. Personal communication.

Index of Clients

General Index

Roman type indicates a brief reference, **bold** type a lengthier discussion.